Warrior
Princess

Put On Your Identity
Pick Up Your Sword

Melinda D. Poitras

Cover Design: Mike Long
Cover Photo: Timothy Eberly & Pro-Church Media
on Unsplash
(Free to use under Unsplash license)

ISBN: 9798835147250

DEDICATION

For Charity,
whose God makes royals
out of slaves.

CONTENTS

1

PRINCESS MATERIAL

I once read an article by an overweight woman. I wish I had flagged it, saved it, written down her name and details for credit, but I didn't. Each time I went to look for it I failed in the finding. I won't forget it though. She wrote about her struggle to find decent work on Broadway. How hard it was, even with a considerable amount of talent, to get a good role due to type casting. What stuck out to me the most was her statement of defeat encapsulating the realization that people would rather believe children could fly out of the window of a nursery to Neverland or baboons could sing power ballads or women could fly in and out of places in a bubble than that someone who looked like her could find love or happiness.

- I'm not saying this is the most uplifting way to begin a book.

- I'm just saying I thought I couldn't be a princess.

- I just naturally assumed I wouldn't fit the part.

This was not ever something I voiced out loud until one fateful Halloween when I dressed as Cruella DeVille for our youth group's fall costume party. I sent my friend Chase a picture. He clapped back hard:

"Why do you always dress as a villain?"

"What do you mean?"

"Don't pretend you don't know what I'm talking about. Basically every time you get an opportunity to dress up, you dress up as a villain of some sort."

"Oh. I'm more believable that way."

"Excuse me?"

"I'm more believable as a villain. I just don't think I can pull off being a princess. I'm just not princess material."

"What are you talking about? You are made of princess material!"

I made him angry. I usually have to try a lot harder to actually accomplish that. The lecture which followed was long and full of encouragement. He clarified for me clearly and concisely that I can, in fact, one hundred percent be believed as a princess. I hung up the phone encouraged, but still unsure. Even if everyone else found me believable as a princess, could I?

Samuel Taylor Coleridge coined the term "suspension of disbelief." Simply put, it refers to the ability of an audience to put aside their own knowledge of the world and how it practically works to immerse themselves in a story. It's the capability to turn off reality for their own enjoyment. For an hour or so readers, listeners, or viewers of a piece of art will believe pixie dust is real or water can take on human form or shape or other things of that sort in order to enjoy a story. Whatever concept is introduced is believed as reality. For that time period, disbelief is simply suspended.

The author and finisher of my faith calls me to my own suspension of disbelief of sorts. The difference is, as He is telling the tale of my life, introducing heroes, expunging villains, making me the heroine I could never be and dressing me in royal rags, every bit of the unbelievable story He's weaving, is true. Romans seven tells us there are two types of law at work:

> *"So I find this law at work: Although I want to do good, evil is right there with me. For in my inner being I delight in God's law; but I see another law at work in me, waging war against the law of my mind and making me a prisoner of the law of sin at work within me. What a wretched man I am! Who will rescue me from this body that is subject to death? Thanks be to God, who delivers me through Jesus Christ our Lord! So then, I myself in my mind am a slave to God's law, but in my sinful nature a slave to the law of sin"*
>
> Romans 7:21-25 (NIV)

Thus far it sounds like an eternal wrestling match we are all too familiar with, but the hope really waltzes into the picture in chapter eight:

> *"You, however, are not in the realm of the flesh but are in the realm of the Spirit, if indeed the Spirit of God lives in you. And if anyone does not have the Spirit of Christ, they do not belong to Christ. But if Christ is in you, then even though your body is subject to death because of sin, the Spirit gives life because of righteousness. And if the Spirit of him who raised Jesus from the dead is living in you, he who raised Christ from the dead will also give life to your mortal bodies because of[e] his Spirit who lives in you. Therefore, brothers and sisters, we have an obligation—but it is not to the flesh, to live according to it. For if you live according to the flesh, you will die; but if by the Spirit you put to death the misdeeds of the body, you will live"*
>
> Romans 8:9-13 (NIV)

We're surrounded by flesh, encased inside of it, living in it, but our lives are not about what we live in, rather they submit to what lives in us. Our Savior lives within us and our obligation is not to the world, the things it proclaims, the principles it follows, or the reality it speaks. We live in this world, but we are far from subject to it.

> *"For those who are led by the Spirit of God are the children of*

God. The Spirit you received does not make you slaves, so that you live in fear again; rather, the Spirit you received brought about your adoption to sonship. And by him we cry, "Abba, Father." The Spirit himself testifies with our spirit that we are God's children. Now if we are children, then we are heirs— heirs of God and co-heirs with Christ, if indeed we share in his sufferings in order that we may also share in his glory"

Romans 8:14-17 (NIV)

When I was young, I loved to go on trips with my father. Going on trips with Dad meant I got to fly in a plane just like he did, eat at the head table just like he did, sit on the platforms in front of all the people just like he did. I was his child. I got what he got. The Lord has made us heirs in Christ. We walk through this earth and face trials and tribulations but in the end – we get what He gets because we are His.

"What, then, shall we say in response to these things? If God is for us, who can be against us? He who did not spare his own Son, but gave him up for us all—how will he not also, along with him, graciously give us all things? Who will bring any charge against those whom God has chosen? It is God who justifies. Who then is the one who condemns? No one. Christ Jesus who died—more than that, who was raised to life—is at the right hand of God and is also interceding for us. Who shall separate us from the love of Christ? Shall trouble or hardship or persecution or famine or nakedness or danger or sword? As it is written: For your sake we face death all day long; we are considered as sheep to be slaughtered.

No, in all these things we are more than conquerors through him who loved us. For I am convinced that neither death nor life, neither angels nor demons, neither the present nor the future, nor any powers, neither height nor depth, nor anything else in all creation, will be able to separate us from the love of God that is in Christ Jesus our Lord,"

Romans 8:31-39 (NIV)

No sword can separate me from the love of my Father, and He has made me more than a conqueror in Him.

The truth is, I don't have to dress up to be a villain. I am that way. I was born that way. My flesh and the Spirit are constantly at war. I wrestle long and hard with all the darkness inside me. Even on days when I've not created a tentacle tutu and dressed myself up as a sea witch, the villain inside me fights hard to be free. My flesh will not reign victorious though. There is an alternate universe my Father is ruler of, a true reality that wins in the end. And when I lean hard into His Word, and take up His work, when I suspend my disbelief and surrender to His ultimate reality, I find that Chase was right all along. I am made of princess material.

I am a princess…

…and a warrior.

2

LITTLE PRINCESSES, LIONS, AND LOW SELF-ESTEEM

Frances Hodgson Burnett wrote a wonderful children's story called "A Little Princess." It tells of a young girl named Sara who, though wealthy, is kind and good in all of her ways. She is sent to live at a boarding school where she is doted upon and favored until a twist of misfortune renders her penniless. She is banished to poor living quarters, treated miserably, and forced to work as a servant. Throughout every misfortune she remains kind and loving to the world around her, giving of herself to help and further the cause of others even as she is being mistreated. The book ends quite differently, but in multiple movie versions her father, who was thought to be lost in the war, ends up living in the house next door. Through a series of events Sara stumbles upon her father at the last minute, and begs him to remember her. He doesn't at first, having suffered from injuries and amnesia, but just as she is being dragged back to her life of misery he races after her and reclaims her as his own. It's a lovely scene, and a beautiful moment, but what is even more beautiful to me is Sara's ability to hold on to her identity no matter her circumstance. She knows who she is. No matter the mistreatment she endures or opposition she comes against, she remembers who she belongs to.

I was growing up in Africa when Disney released *The Lion King*. My favorite part of that famous classic is when Simba

7

looks at his reflection and encounters his father. (A veritable impossibility as his father died several scenes before.) Mufasa tells Simba,

"You've forgotten me."

Simba argues with him, saying he could never forget his father. Mufasa admonishes that when Simba forgets who he is, he also forgets who his father is.

"Remember who you are," he reminds his son as he vanishes into mist.

"Remember who you are."

I have noticed, more often than not, when we are struggling to find our own identities and we are tossed about on the whims and waves of someone else's acceptance or opinion, it's because we've forgotten who we are as well.

Sadie Robertson explores this concept of our identity in Christ, as it relates to *The Lion King*, even further, in a speech she gives. She mentions Simba returning to the Pride Lands to confront Scar and save his people. She asks,

"What does Scar say, when he hears Simba let out that roar?"

That's right, he says, "Mufasa," because when Simba steps back into his destiny and returns to his rightful place of authority, to his enemy he sounds just like his Dad."

That's who we are. Children of the King. Warrior princesses meant to stand, and fight, and sound just like our father.

We have this joke at home that my sister is a daddy's girl, but I am my father's son. I write books and I speak and it's a big deal to me to carry on his legacy as far as his life's work goes. My sister looks just like him and they have the same personality and together their type A attitude makes me insane. But in my work, and my life philosophy, and what I do with my time and my money, I am just like him.

I love being a writer like my daddy. I love it when people tell me I speak like my daddy. And all this year, any time I read the Bible, it keeps standing out to me "the Lord God of armies." It's not just in one book of the Bible, everywhere I read it's popping out at me "the Lord God of armies."

I read verses like this: *"The Lord is a man of war; the Lord is his name"* (Exodus 15:3) and I realize, my Father, God, is a King, which makes me a princess. But He's also a warrior, and that makes me a girl with a sword.

I cannot separate my DNA from that of my earthly father's, and I cannot separate who I am from who I am in Christ.

This is a good thing because, quite frankly, I don't have any more self-esteem.

There it is. I've reached the end of it.

I'm generally a very confident person so this whole situation is unusual and frightening and somewhat humorous. I was describing it to my sister:

> "I feel completely worthless. I mean, it's ridiculous. I walk out the door and I don't know why anyone would even want to talk to me. I sit down to write and I struggle with whether or not I even have anything to say. I have so much to change and so much to do and so much that I put so much stock in was a total lie that I don't even want anyone to see me. Not like this. Is this… Canj. Is this low self-esteem?!?"

She laughed at me.

My self-esteem has defied ridiculous odds in the past. I

shouldn't have had any and I almost had too much. My Dad would comment on it all the time: "We don't even know how this is happening. But you're somehow confident." (He's the cutest person ever.)

No matter what anyone has said or done my entire life (which has been quite a lot of saying and doing) I've always been like

"That's nice guys, I'm going to go ahead and be awesome anyway. Thanks." And now I'm more like "You're right. You were always right. Allow me to lie here and die." And I mean it. It's been ridiculous.

One morning not too long ago, I read this passage in Job:

> *"Behold, thou hast instructed many, and thou hast strengthened the weak hands. Thy words have upheld him that was falling, and thou hast strengthened the feeble knees. But now it is come upon thee, and thou faintest; it toucheth thee, and thou art troubled."*

Job 4:3-5 (KJV)

I saw myself too clearly in those verses. I left the room, went into my bedroom, and had a complete breakdown. Shaking, crying, trouble breathing – major panic attack.

"Lord, you're going to have to help me because in fifteen minutes I have to leave this house and witness to a handful of people who need you. I've got nothing. I am nothing. You're going to have to help me so much as breathe." That was all said, mentally I think, because I couldn't talk.

I told my friend Joe about it the next day and he simply inquired:

"Isn't that something one of Job's stupid friends said?"

He was right. It was. Here's the thing about my self-esteem. It's fickle as can be. Because it is based on self. Here is another thing about self-esteem: Ultimately, I don't need it. I don't need good self-esteem. I don't need bad

10

self-esteem. I don't need high self-esteem. I don't need low self- esteem. You know what I need to be esteeming?

God.

Because if I'm truly esteeming God, I will accomplish what He wants me to do, no matter how I feel about myself, and He will give me the strength to do so. Period. I mean, just look at it. High self-esteem:

> "**I'm** pretty awesome. **I** don't think **I'm** amazing or anything but **I** do okay. **I'm** all right. If **I** need to get something done these are the ways that **I** accomplish it. If **I** need to turn to my friends they are there for **me** and if **I** need love and support **I** know where to get it. **I'm** pretty blessed. **I'm** doing pretty good."

Low self-esteem:

> "**I** am absolutely worthless. **I** have nothing going for me. **I** always fail at everything that **I** try. **I** attempt to love people- they don't love **me** back. **I** attempt to do **my** best – **my** best is mediocre. **I** am failure at life and **I** have nowhere to turn."

Low self-esteem, high self-esteem, they are vastly different but they share some common ground don't they? **Self. There is an awful lot of self in self-esteem**.

I know this man; greatest man that you could ever meet or wish to meet. He's been through a lot in his life. A lot, a lot. Stuff you could never even imagine a lot. And ever since I've known him, he's been changing the world. Consistently, passionately, visibly, changing the world. He has had every reason to give up. He has had every reason to quit, but he never does. And he never will. He could sit around thinking about all the things that he has tried that have failed. All the things that he has done that have gone unappreciated. All of the people he has loved who have turned out to be lame. But he doesn't. He persists in being the perfect model of an active Christian. Daily. His self-esteem? I'll tell you a secret. It's not that great. Though he's one of the most perfect individuals I have yet to come across, his sense of self-worth can at best be described as "poor." He excels without self-worth. Why? He doesn't need it. Neither do you.

I'm not saying that high self-esteem is a bad thing, or that low self-esteem is not crippling. I know better. Our self is a part of who we are. (Obviously.) I'm just saying, he taught me that there is a time to stop licking your wounds and to go out and get some new ones for the cause of Christ.

> "We don't have time to get it all together before we reach a lost and dying world. People need us now."
>
> Kristin Keller

This wasn't fun to share, but I know it is for someone today. Someone whose pride is not their problem. Maybe you don't need to get over yourself. But you do need to get over your self-esteem.

This isn't a *"feel good, I have all the answers, yippee hooray"* chapter. It's more of an *"I stopped crying and walked out the door still feeling like dirt and was given the strength to minister to some people who don't mind dirt that much, because they literally live in it. Maybe I'll get my confidence back tomorrow, and maybe it will be next week, or maybe I never will. But no matter my level of self-confidence, I should always maintain confidence in He who cannot fail"* reminder.

A reminder that no matter the healthy or unhealthy level of pride with which you view yourself, there's an awful lot of "self" in self-esteem. Who we are only ever matters as it pertains to who He is.

Which is good news, because who we are, is His.

3

THE SIGNIFICANCE OF SLEEPING BEAUTY

I'm not sure what it is that captivates me about the story of Sleeping Beauty. I am a fifth-grade teacher and sometimes I do wonder if it has to do with the deep longing for a nap. Of course it would be nice, I think at times, if a handsome stranger ran into me in the woods and danced with me "once upon a dream," but not as nice as being able to take a good long snooze in peace and silence. When I think about this story, I think about misunderstood villains, gifts from fairies, and princes cutting through brush and briar with incredibly shiny swords but I also cannot help but think of the significance one individual life can have on the world around us.

Think about it, this girl grows up in the forest surrounded by the woodland creatures she loves until one day she wanders into a castle, stumbles into a dark room in a tower and pricks her finger on a spindle. She falls into a deep sleep, but so does the rest of the kingdom.

One girl pricks her finger on a needle, and an entire kingdom falls asleep. So often we fail to realize the impact we have on others. Everything you do changes the life of someone else. You cannot even inhale or exhale without literally changing the atmosphere around you. You can go about your day making normal choices and doing regular things all while having absolutely no idea you are affecting the world around you.

When I was in my early teens I went through a literary phase where I was absolutely obsessed with the romanticism of brushing my hair one hundred times through a day. I had seen or read somewhere that doing so made your hair more glossy and likely to shine. (In all honesty, I had a perm. So I'm not sure what I was thinking but am not ashamed to admit to you this practice was not at all effective. It basically cultivated a level of frizz unparalleled elsewhere on the planet, but I was one hundred percent consistent with it). I would brush my hair one hundred times through faithfully every night. One day I passed my tiny visiting cousin in the hallway as she was playing with her Barbies. She was ministering to Barbie's tangled locks with the customary plastic brush as she said the words:

"Hang in there Barbie. It's a good practice to brush your hair one hundred times through each night. It makes it shiny."

I had not sat my cousin down for a tutorial on proper hair brushing practice. (Although, as long as we're being honest, such a move would not have been at all unlike me). I did not show her flash cards or drill this thought into her. She had just noticed. Being around me had impacted her thoughts on life, albeit in a small and insignificant way.

The little things we do matter. When I look at Scripture I think about all the things that would have been different if people had not given their all to simple and seemingly miniscule tasks or practices.

Elisha says to the widow woman in 2 Kings 4:2, "What do you have in your house?"

A woman who had lost her husband to death, ran the risk of losing her two sons to debt. The prophet asked her what she had in her house. All she had was a jar of oil. He instructed her to borrow as many containers as she could get her hands on. I'm sure the woman did not fully comprehend why it was important and necessary for her to borrow so many containers from her neighbors. But she did what she was asked immediately and efficiently, gathering as many containers as she and her sons were able to get her hands on, doing what she knew to do to the best of her ability. When she was instructed to pour her jar of oil into the containers she must have been amazed to notice the oil wasn't running out. She was able to fill every single vessel she had borrowed and sell the oil to cancel her debts. She thought she was just gathering cups, bottles, and bowls, but really, she was securing her future.

Genesis chapter 24 finds Rebekah at a well. She had come to do the daily chore of fetching water when a man asked her for a drink. She had no way of knowing her offer of watering all his camels as well as quenching his own thirst would land her with the perfect husband God intended. She was just being herself. She was practicing the tenants of her normal character, going about her regular everyday tasks. She didn't know the servant had prayed specifically. He hadn't known what to look for with his eyes, but he had asked to be shown a clear picture of the heart of Isaac's future wife. Rebekah fit the bill, just by being herself. She passed the test by practicing her regular routine.

Before we experience the miracle of the loaves and fishes in Matthew 14, somebody's mother packs a lunch. How was the little boy's mother to know when she packed him up for his day out she was actually providing food for 5,000 people? She just faithfully did what she knew to do and unknowingly impacted the world.

I love the example of significance being tied to a seemingly insignificant thing that we find in 2 Kings.

"Now Elisha had been suffering from the illness from which he

died. Jehoash king of Israel went down to see him and wept over him. 'My father! My father!' he cried. 'The chariots and horsemen of Israel!' Elisha said, 'Get a bow and some arrows,' and he did so. 'Take the bow in your hands,' he said to the king of Israel. When he had taken it, Elisha put his hands on the king's hands. 'Open the east window,' he said, and he opened it. 'Shoot!' Elisha said, and he shot. 'The LORD's arrow of victory, the arrow of victory over Aram!' Elisha declared. 'You will completely destroy the Arameans at Aphek.' Then he said, 'Take the arrows,' and the king took them. Elisha told him, 'Strike the ground.' He struck it three times and stopped. The man of God was angry with him and said, 'You should have struck the ground five or six times; then you would have defeated Aram and completely destroyed it. But now you will defeat it only three times,'

2 Kings 13: 14-19 (NIV)

Here the king is, in the face of crisis, being asked to perform a seemingly meaningless task. He has no idea when he is striking the ground with arrows he is actually deciding the fate of his kingdom in battle. I love to use that passage when I am speaking to parents. I pair it with Psalm 127:4-5:

"Like arrows in the hands of a warrior are children born in one's youth. Blessed is the man whose quiver is full of them. They will not be put to shame when they contend with their opponents in court."

It may feel like you're just changing diapers or making breakfast or tucking tiny toes into bed on a loop but really, you are raising weapons of mass destruction for the kingdom of God with what is in your house already. You are vital to the kingdom, you are significant to the story, this is why its important to do whatever task you find at hand with commitment and excellence.

"Whatever your hand finds to do, do it with all your might,"
Ecclesiastes 9:10

One of my first Christmases living in America, I found myself burdened for the janitorial staff at the World Headquarters building of the United Pentecostal Church International. I just couldn't get away from the horrible thought they might clean our building but never experience the love of Christ or hear the gospel. I didn't know what to do about that. I wasn't sure there was anything I could do about that. I prayed and I really felt prompted to make cupcakes. I am no great baker, but I took care in making these cupcakes. I used my grandmother's recipe and I made them from scratch. I made red velvet, chocolate, and butternut cupcakes. I bought cute cupcake paper and fun containers to put the cupcakes in. I crafted a message with care, included an invitation to our church's Christmas candlelight service, and tied the whole affair up with ribbons. Heart pounding, I walked into the building to deliver this labor of baked from scratch love.

I could not locate one solitary member of the janitorial staff. Not one of them was in the building. Despondent and defeated, I left the love offering in the janitorial office with a note detailing how I hoped they knew they were valued and appreciated.

I thought about these cupcakes a lot. Did anyone even find them before they went stale? How much of a difference would it have made if they had? What was I even thinking? Was it even okay to leave gifts in the janitorial office or was this some inappropriate form of "come to my church" bribery?

I wasn't sure I would ever know. Months passed and no-one ever mentioned the cupcakes. I assumed someone found them before they became a rat party but maybe not. Also, who am I to judge? Maybe the rats really needed a party that Christmas.

I was thrilled to hear the news that Ryan O'Neil had prayed a janitorial worker through to the Holy Ghost in our chapel one day. My cupcakes had long since succumbed to whatever fate had met them, but my heart for the people in our building hearing the good news for themselves still beat strong. It made me smile to know the Lord had met this prayer of my heart, even if He hadn't used me to do it. My mother came home from the office a few days later with news to tell me. She said she had met the woman, the woman who had come to the Lord. She told her how happy she was to hear about her experience in the chapel. The woman said that it was the most beautiful experience of her life and she was so thankful. The next phrase out of her mouth was totally unexpected:

"Oh, and Sis. Poitras? Please thank your daughter. Thank her so much for the note and the cupcakes. She can't know what they meant."

> "So neither the one who plants nor the one who waters is anything, but only God, who makes things grow"
>
> 1 Corinthians 3:7

I don't know what the outcome of your every action will be, but I do know your every action is significant. You are known, loved, and chosen by a heavenly Father who has created you to make an impact on this world, and you are making an impact on this world in ways you do not understand or see. Like a stone falling into a lake or a butterfly flapping its wings, the effect of all you do ripples out across the river.

You just go wherever He leads. You just do whatever He tells you to do. Gather containers. Water camels. Pack lunches. Make cupcakes. Change the world.

4

NO DAMSEL IN DISTRESS

One of my favorite people was having a baby, and from the very first moment we were nuts about this kid. Her husband walked into a conversation we were having, and told us how someone had asked, at lunch, if they wanted children. He had said he wasn't sure about the timing yet. When he walked out of the room I looked at her and said,

"I'm pretty sure you're already pregnant." She was. Immediately, I was all about this baby, I'm telling you. It was to the point that I came home from Greece instead of journeying on to Rome in order to avoid missing the baby shower and I almost never regret it unless I see a really good picture of the Trevi Fountain. It was the happiest secret and the best time of dreaming and scheming with the Lord. We would get out notebooks and compare notes with each other:

"This is what the Lord has been saying to me about the baby, what has He been saying to you?" One of the major things we felt about the baby was that he would be a boy. I felt this so strongly. I was incredibly confident in this fact right up until the day of the gender reveal when I pulled a pink top out of the closet.

Baby's dad let an arrow fly towards a target and pink powder exploded everywhere. We were getting a girl. Eventually, I asked the Lord,

"I'm not complaining, thank You Jesus for this life, but I was so sure she would be a boy. I really felt it strongly, what was going on with that?" He replied:

"I allowed you to sense the presence of a mighty warrior in the womb. You are the one who assigned that warrior a gender."

She's my angel baby. She's the happiest, cutest, cuddliest little thing. She is independent, but always seems to know when I've had a bad day, laying across my heart like the perfect emotional band-aid no matter how much she'd rather be running in play. We also really have to watch her because she will jump off of, climb up on, run into absolutely everything if we're not careful. One of the first things she began to do was growl. She growls with great ferocity and sass. What a little lioness. What a mighty warrior already. The Lord put her in the right house too, because it was her mother who said to me,

"It's not enough to just put on your princess crown. You also have to pick up your sword."

My angel baby's mother, she just won't let me stay down.

One day Jesus was teaching, and Pharisees and teachers of the law were sitting there. They had come from every village of Galilee and from Judea and Jerusalem. And the power of the Lord was with Jesus to heal the sick. Some men came carrying a paralyzed man on a mat and tried to take him into the house to lay him before Jesus. When they could not find a way to do this because of the crowd, they went up on the roof and lowered him on his mat through the tiles into the middle of the crowd, right in front of Jesus. When Jesus saw their faith, he said,

"Friend, your sins are forgiven." Luke 5:17-20

I love this verse so much because a man had friends who knew they had to get him to Jesus. They wouldn't stop at anything, no obstacle could deter them. Then, when Jesus saw their faith, he said to the paralyzed man "your sins are forgiven." Which He followed by healing his infirmity. When he couldn't get there himself, his friends carried him to Jesus. When he was paralyzed, hurting, and in need of help, their faith made him truly whole.

I woke up during the night in Greece, before returning home for the baby shower. I sat straight up in bed, knowing something was wrong. It turns out my friend had been in a car accident. She was completely fine, but I remember the fury that rushed through me at the thought harm would come anywhere near my beautiful person carrying such precious life. I prayed until the Lord reassured me, nothing would be able to touch her. It was true then. It is true now. The enemy absolutely cannot touch this friend of mine. So he whispers lies instead. Unable to lay a hand on her, her torments her with falsehood. This, we combat with the Word of God. I have no other friend who struggles as much with the lies of the enemy, and I have no other friend who is as successful and faithful in fighting those same satanic whispers off of my own life. She lifts her shield of faith to defend me often, with her skilled sword she slices through the doubt I am trapped by all the time.

John Bunyan wrote about a pilgrim on a journey. His name was Christian, and he and his companion were headed for The Celestial City. Somewhere along the way they encountered a storm which confused their direction and covered the signs with mud. They ended up falling captive to a giant called Despair. He took them to his home, Doubting Castle where they were introduced to his wife, Diffidence, which means "low self-esteem". Every day he would beat them before taking them to look at the bones of all the others who had fallen prey to his traps. Every day he told them he would kill them, that they would never make it out of his castle alive. He didn't actually do it, he just promised he would, over and over and over. One day, as they were discussing things between themselves, Christian and his companion thought:

> *"Didn't Evangelist give us a key? I wonder if it would work on any of these locks?" They give it a try and the key does in fact open every single lock in the castle as they make a great escape."*

The Word of God opens prison doors. It always has. It always will.

Maybe you need a friend like mine today, a companion on this journey, so allow me to be that for you.

Woman. You are called by God, hand crafted for the work He intends for you to do. You are loved and anointed, sought after and cherished. You are made in His image and beautiful in His sight. Put on that tiara! But it's not enough to just put on your tiara, you have to pick up your sword. You are a mighty warrior, a lioness arising, a gift to this kingdom. Pick up your sword and fight. Fight for your peace of mind. Fight for your family. Fight for His promises until you see them come to pass. Endure until the end, knowing full well what lies in store.

Here is a glimpse of that for you. Your story ends just like Pilgrim's Progress does.

Christian and his friend make it over the Enchanted ground and enter into the country of Beulah. The air there is fresh, refreshing, pleasant, and they are able to take rest in all the beauty around them. Every day they see new flowers appear and they hear birds, specifically turtle doves, constantly singing.

> *"Thou shalt no more be termed Forsaken; neither shall thy land any more be termed Desolate:*
>
> *but thou shalt be called Hephzibah, (my delight is in that one) and thy land Beulah: for the LORD delighteth in thee, and thy land shall be married,"*

Isaiah 62:4

"My beloved spake, and said unto me, Rise up, my love, my fair one, and come away. For, lo, the winter is past, the rain is over and gone; The flowers appear on the earth; the time of the singing of birds is come, and the voice of the turtle is heard in our land,"

Song of Solomon 2:10-12

"In this country the sun shineth night and day; wherefore this was beyond the Valley of the Shadow of Death, and also out of the reach of Giant Despair, neither could they from this place so much as see Doubting Castle."[1]

Take out your key, unlock your prison, and shake off despair. You may be down, but you are no damsel in distress.

---

[1] Pilgrim's Progress – John Bunyan

5

INHERITANCE GUARANTEED

Louisa May Alcott, the author of *Little Women* and *Good Wives*, wrote a lesser known story by the name of *Inheritance*. In it, a beautiful young girl named Edith lives as a ward within a family, loved and treasured, but still often treated as a second-class citizen. She discovers she is actually the heir to all the family owns on the eve of the death of the family patriarch. He tells her she is really his niece, and gives her the documentation to back up her claim to her inheritance. Wishing for nothing to change, she burns the documents, content to live in the family's house, keeping things the way they are.

A jealous rival, seeking to displace her from the family's good graces, accuses her of stealing, planting evidence that she is a thief. Edith proclaims her innocence over and over and, at the last moment, the real thief bursts back onto the scene. Edith had always been kind to him so when he saw her burning the documents he rescued them from the fire and kept them for the right time. He confesses his guilt and proves Edith is the true heir to all the family's fortune. The mother asked why she would do such a thing, why she would ever think of hiding this information. Edith responds that she didn't want anything to change.

"Take it Edith," the line is delivered, charged with love, admiration, and emotion, "It's your inheritance."

Before I began writing this book a trusted man of God called and began to speak:

> "Twice in Melinda's life she has fought for her inheritance. She has fought for her inheritance and through God she has prevailed. She wasn't always aware of what was in the envelope. She wasn't always certain her name was even on it. But she fought and she prevailed. That inheritance now detaches and becomes a foundation for ministry. A foundation for a building that the Lord will use."

Allow me to speak it now, write it clear, yell it loud. I hope this cry reaches to your ear drums and your heart and that it crawls into your very spirit and it does not let go.

What is for you, is for you. There is no reason to fear. There is no reason to doubt. There is no reason to worry. What is for you, is for you. Your inheritance is yours.

> *"Do not be afraid, little flock, for your Father has been pleased to give you the kingdom."*
>
> Luke 12:32 (NIV)

You are a child and an heir. At the end of the day, no matter what, you have been given an inheritance, and you will have what is yours.

There may come a time when you feel the lack of almost everything you deem necessary. There will not be enough. You will not be enough, and somehow you will still feel like you're too much. Endure.

You may be so sleep deprived that you are walking about in an ironic dream stupor. Endure.

The promises of God may FaceTime you. You know, close enough to see clearly, close enough to interact with but not close enough to hold. Endure.

You may dial the exact number you need only to be placed on hold for hours. Listen to the elevator music and endure.

You may put on the tailormade calling of God only to realize that things that fit like a glove are not always comfortable. Endure.

Other people's happy, it gets loud, no matter how much you love them. It's okay to plug your ears. It's okay to hug your own heart a minute. Endure.

You can throw parties everyone kills to come to and they'll still forget to invite you to theirs. Endure.

Harboring hope is dangerous, promises are perilous fugitives. They could cost you your life, but seeing them through to safety might change the world. It might even change *your* world. Endure.

Breathe deep. Keep a list of gratitude. Send the text, show up to the Starbucks, write the note, make the call, ask the questions, buy the confetti, drive in the rain, dance. Dance like David or Dora the Explorer when she achieves a victory or like donuts are in your future because donuts are in fact, in your future. Endure.

Do it tired. Do it scared. Do it for Jesus and your people and you. Endure.

Remember, nothing lasts forever. Sigh of relief.

Nothing lasts forever. Hold on tight.

No matter how bad a day is it contains beauty you will never ever get back. Find it. Embrace it. Endure.

Life is full of harsh realities you cannot change. Acknowledge them, release them, endure.

Life is beautiful. There is a reason today is called a "present." He's doing all the things He's promised even if we can't find them amid the wrapping paper. Endure.

He is good. Endure.

Love is worth it. Endure.

Life is beautiful, all the pieces, every hour, even pain – so endure.

The fastest runners don't always win the race and the strongest warriors don't always win the battle. Time and chance happen to all but He stands outside of time and leaves nothing up to chance, so endure.

I'll say it again. I'll say it for me yesterday, for us today, and for you tomorrow. I'm serious. Buy the confetti. You are going to need it.

Endure until the end, and be saved. Saved, and so. much. more.

6

MIRROR MIRROR

There's a fairy tale about a beautiful woman who would stand in front of her mirror, where I have noticed beautiful women do like to stand. She says a rhyme while she stands there:

"Magic mirror, on the wall, who's the fairest one of all?"

The mirror answers day after day with what the queen wants most to hear, that she is the most beautiful in the land. This continues until the day Snow White comes of age and surpasses the queen in beauty, provoking her to fly into a vengeful rage. She becomes consumed with eradicating this threat to her status, and hires a henchman to kill the innocent girl.

All of this for beauty, an ideal that's not even that useful. It's not like it is sustenance. It's not like you can eat it.

You can't eat beauty.

If you could, I honestly think I would pay a lot more attention to it.

I'm not being glib – I'm serious.

"You can't eat beauty."

My Deandra said this phrase to me the other day. She said it because I was curled up in a ball at the very bottom of my parent's empty bed, huddled underneath the covers.

She said it to get me to come out into the world again. I had just had an exceptionally good cry and when I was done, she called me and I told her:

> "Jen, I don't know how I'm supposed to do this. If XYZ cannot be happy because she is not pretty enough, if 123 cannot appreciate what she has, if 2B8L cannot ever accept herself the way that she is, I do not know how I with all of my weight and worry and wondering am supposed to even get out of bed. I don't know how to function."

She reminded me that I could, in fact, function because open approval and outward perfection are not what is ultimately important. (It is usually me giving that particular lecture). She told me to watch a speech by Lupita Nyongo and I did. I watched an unbelievably stunning woman talk about how old she was when she began to realize that just maybe, on some distant planet, it might be okay that she was darker than most everyone else around her. How a dark-skinned model arrived on the scene and everyone called her beautiful and so Lupita thought she might have to accept that she could possibly be beautiful too but that she "wanted to reject it because she had begun to enjoy the seduction of inadequacy." How even though this model was on the world's stage and the "distant gate keepers of beauty" had approved of her the preference around Lupita still leaned toward lighter skin. How her mother had told her:

"You can't eat beauty. It doesn't feed you." And how when she said this she meant that "you can't rely on how you look to sustain you. What actually sustains you, what is fundamentally beautiful is compassion – for yourself and for those around you. That kind of beauty inflames the heart and enchants the soul."

I was in the car the other day with some friends and I looked at a picture and I said:

"I love standing next to Caleb because he makes me feel short."

And there's this boy who eventually becomes my brother-in-law and who is also only one in a million and only one of the best things that ever happened to me and he said:

"What are you talking about?"

"You know, Caleb's so tall, it makes me feel short."

"You are short."

"I'm really not that…"

"Mel. You're short."

"I don't really know why you think this because I've never really thought of myself as…

"MELINDA. **I don't know who has been measuring you, or who you have been measuring yourself against** but you really are quite short."

(How the Lord leads him in even his casual conversation actually astounds me because tomorrow, he is just as likely to be telling me I'm tall if for some reason that is what I need to hear. Friends are not only the family you choose but the family the Lord chooses for you.)

There was a nail there that's been snagging up my confidence and he hit it. Honestly, I'm average height. I'm right in the middle of the spectrum. And I have legitimately been walking around overly self-conscious because I'm so tall.

The crazy thing is – it's not even my insecurity. It's someone else's.

I picked up someone else's insecurity and I have been carrying it.

That was the moment that I truly realized:

31

If you can't eat beauty, you can't feed anyone else with it either. How much you weigh, or how tall you are, or if you follow the fashion trends, or if your eyebrows are plucked, or if your hair looks good that day – that doesn't sustain you and it sure as all that is holy doesn't sustain anyone else.

I'm not saying that it's okay to let yourself go. I'm not saying you're not accountable for how you take care of your body. I'm not saying I don't go to bed crying about how I'm crying about not being able to eat pizza when there are children who don't get to eat. I'm not saying that you shouldn't be convicted or that it's not okay to be cute or that you shouldn't shower and you should eat yourself into oblivion because "everyone is beautiful."

This is what I'm saying:

What makes you beautiful is not how you look.

What makes you beautiful is not how many people are standing by to confirm and affirm and reaffirm said beauty.

Beauty isn't about being fed. It's about who you are and who that is feeding.

I am saying that there are these gorgeous women (inside and out) who are changing my life. Like Annie Downs who blogged that she frankly "doesn't feel pretty in Africa" the day that she's headed there anyway. Like Miriam Henson who posted on Facebook that she tries not to criticize herself so that her daughter will be spared from beauty issues as long as possible. (The same daughter who thinks her mother is insanely beautiful. The same daughter who is right about that). Like the (in)courage blogger who once wrote the best thing you can do for someone else is to "eat the cookie" **because a refusal to accept yourself is always a rejection of others**. Like brave, black, and truly beautiful Lupita Nyongo who urges us to "feel the validation of external beauty but also, get to the deeper business of being beautiful inside."

I am saying the point is not at all that I am short or tall, the point is in the measuring. That same measuring the Bible blatantly calls stupid in 2 Corinthians 10:12. What if I just. stopped. measuring? What if I just stopped allowing others to add me up and subtract me down, simply by ignoring their math? Because no math could ever measure the sum total of a person.

I am saying that when Jesus tells Peter: "Get thee behind me Satan" (Matthew 16:23) He only ever said it because Peter was "savoring not the things that be of God, but those that be of men." And if I work hard all day, and I love the Lord, and I serve His people and He is as close as the mention of His name and I walk with Him throughout the day and then I go to bed and cry because not enough people confirmed that I am pretty (or smart, or competent, or a good daughter, or a good friend) – **what am I savoring then?**

I am saying that it might be a good idea, just maybe, to spend a little less time worrying about my reflection and a little more time **reflecting Light**.

Today, I will comb my hair. I will. I will try my hardest not to look like I have crawled out of a dumpster. Of course. I'll have something low in caloric content for lunch and work out and maybe even Nair my upper lip. But none of that will ever profit me anything if I don't get down to the deeper business of being beautiful inside.

Because you can't eat beauty. And **God forbid that anyone ever leave my house hungry**.

Back to the evil queen in the story of Snow White for a moment. You know what's so interesting to me? She's not looking in the mirror to admire her own features or understand her own flaws, she's not interested in what her reflection has to say about her. She's worried about what her reflection has to say as compared to someone else's.

> *"We do not dare to classify or compare ourselves with some who commend themselves. When they measure themselves by themselves and compare themselves with themselves, they are not wise."*
>
> 2 Corinthians 10:12 (NIV)

Not only was it a lack of wisdom to measure her beauty by someone else's, it was borderline insanity. This woman cared so much about being the most beautiful in the land she was willing to shed innocent blood to maintain her status. And to what end? What would this wasteful sacrifice even accomplish? It would not have been successful, even without true love's kiss added to the mixture and reversing the effects of the poison apple. There would always have been someone else to threaten her, some other face to overshadow her own, some other force to be reckoned with. Measuring ourselves against each other is always a lack of wisdom, and we want to be wise girls. What does a wise girl even look like?

To answer this question I am drawn to a specific portion of Scripture:

> *"At that time the kingdom of heaven will be like ten virgins who took their lamps and went out to meet the bridegroom. Five of them were foolish and five were wise. The foolish ones took their lamps but did not take any oil with them. The wise ones, however, took oil in jars along with their lamps. The bridegroom was a long time in coming, and they all became drowsy and fell asleep. At midnight the cry rang out:*
>
> *'Here's the bridegroom! Come out to meet him!' Then all the virgins woke up and trimmed their lamps. The foolish ones said to the wise,*
>
> *'Give us some of your oil; our lamps are going out.'*
>
> *'No,' they replied, 'there may not be enough for both us and*

you. Instead, go to those who sell oil and buy some for yourselves.' But while they were on their way to buy the oil, the bridegroom arrived. The virgins who were ready went in with him to the wedding banquet. And the door was shut. Later the others also came.

'Lord, Lord,' they said, 'open the door for us!' But he replied,

'Truly I tell you, I don't know you.'

Therefore keep watch, because you do not know the day or the hour,"

Matthew 25:1-13 (NIV)

This parable is meant to illustrate the importance of you guarding your own salvation, and ultimately is written in reference to the Kingdom of Heaven and how to enter it. I think there's a principal here for stewarding our self-esteem and dealing with the concept of beauty as well.

When the time came for the bridegroom to appear, none of the girls were able to help each other or share their oil. At the end of the day it all came down to what was inside their own lamps. At the end of the day when you are called upon to serve others, to minister in the kingdom, to tear down strongholds or build up hearts or encourage lives, you will be operating with your own oil. You cannot borrow from your neighbor, you cannot run to the store at the last minute. What you have going on inside of you with Jesus is what is going to count in the end.

I think often of the Brothers Grimm version of the story of Cinderella. It is a much more graphic telling than what we experience from Disney. When the glass slipper arrives at the house her stepsisters rush to the door and begin doing anything they can to make the slipper fit. They end up slashing and cutting their own feet in order to shove them into someone else's shoes.

Understand me: You have shoes made just for you. A path the Lord has lined out for your specific footsteps. Your gifts, your callings, your anointing oil – those things are just for you. You will have what is for you, your name is already on it. There is no need to compare yourself to other's or question your destiny or worry about His intentions.

His intentions are for you. They are for your good. They are to prosper and give you a purpose. And His attention is on you. The light of His life, the love of His heart.

You are the apple of His eye.

And that apple is not poisoned.

You can't eat beauty, and you can't feed anyone with it, but you can live in a palace.

You can live in a palace because you are a princess.

My own home is a palace. Here I serve excessive amounts of chicken and rice, and sweet tea, and bacon, and Tetley, and the Lord.

The cute napkins and the good dishes and the brownies do not matter if I do not also serve the Lord.

And God forbid that anyone ever leave my house hungry.

7

PRINCESS SHOES OF PEACE

Dearest A:

We have spent a great deal of time recently remarking and reminiscing over the many troubles that letters can cause a person. Bab, the Sub-Deb, knows this truth quite well. Yet, she never seems to really learn it. Neither do I. Consequently, I write this to you today.

You have grown up so beautifully, A. So very beautifully. I am grateful that I got to be here to see it.

That's not what I'm writing about though. I am writing about the incident that occurred this Monday. We were watching Anastasia, and Dmitri was about to purchase his train ticket when he looked down at the rose in his pocket. He remembered her, and of course, he couldn't do it. If Paris held the key to her heart, then he would stay in Paris. (Also, someone had to save her from sudden death...) During this time, you sat up, and with great emphasis and passion declared "This will be you, unnamed member of the OPPOSITE SEX (I capitalize as Bab does) this will be you." And that's when I said it. That awful sentence:

"Life is not a Disney movie A."

Has Satan ever been so effective at molding my mouth into his instrument?

Seriously. Somewhere in a meadow a thousand fairies dropped dead.

Since when do I, who abhor cynicism and the application of any kind of realism to dreams in general, say things like that?

Anastasia isn't even a Disney movie!

The point is, it was wrong of me.

It was really wrong of me.

I write now to apologize.

Life is like a Disney movie *for three important reasons.*

1.) *In life, just like in a Disney movie, you are guaranteed trouble. You have run-ins with sharp objects (Sleeping Beauty), Evil plots your demise (The Princess and the Frog), you fight with your father (Aladdin), you lose your shoes (Cinderella), you are separated from home and don't fit in (A Little Mermaid), you must go into hiding (Snow White and the Seven Dwarves), the one you love is determined to make a man out of you (Mulan), you're being pushed into relationships you don't want (Pocahontas), love is literally outlawed (Robin Hood), you get thrown into a dungeon and yelled at (Beauty and the Beast); the list goes on. Trouble = guaranteed. Every single time.* **Keep singing.**

2.) *In life, just like a Disney movie, there is always a lesson to be learned. Every single moment is teaching you something. Some lessons are easy, some hard. Some obvious, some hidden. Some helpful, some a hindrance. Leave your eyes open. Eat the meat. Spit out the bones.* **Keep singing.**

3.) *In life, just like in a Disney movie, dreams do come true. They do. No matter how long it takes. No matter how dark it gets. No matter how hard it is. "If you keep on believing" dreams do come true. Because your dreams? The Lord is writing them. Your dreams are in His hands. Your God; He's something to believe in.* **Keep singing.**

I watched your sister waltz around the kitchen on a day when many wouldn't have felt like dancing and I realized:

*No matter how you feel, there is not a day in your life when you should not also feel like dancing. Because Love is all around you, straight inside you, **present**, all along.*

*I never should have said it A, and I didn't really mean it. "Hope" is your middle name. Literally. It suits you. I pray that rings true your entire lifetime. I pray you're always strong enough to hope and remain unapologetic for it. That you always feel like dancing, no matter how you feel. That you always think that life is like a Disney movie, **because it is**. How does that song go? "These heroes come and go" but let the Lord write this screenplay and you will always find yourself the heroine of something truly epic.*

This I promise you.

This I know.

Keeping singing,

M

P.S: If, when you read this, you wouldn't mind clapping boisterously and letting out a confident "I do believe in Fairies! I do! I do!" You know, just in case I really killed them.

* * *

This letter matters so much to me because of the place I wrote it from. This was a season in my life where I was learning faith and optimism are two entirely different animals. When my heart got broken, my dreams got crushed, my plans failed again and again, my rose-colored glasses slipped from my face and to the ground with a frightful crunching noise. Sound dimmed, color faded, joy was harder to experience and distinguish. I, the girl who loved to sing and dance as if dwelling in her own real-life musical daily was instantaneously and effectively dissuaded from hope. There was no bright side to look on. There was no sun breaking through the horizon. There was little left to be positive about. So I thought my faith was failing. What I failed to realize for the longest stretch of time was

39

that faith and optimism were not the same thing.

Faith doesn't know how things are going to work out. Faith doesn't feel like everything is coming up roses all the time. Faith doesn't hold its breath for happy endings, or pixie dust promises, or "keep fingers crossed that all hopes and dreams will lead to a fairy tale future." Faith is steady trust in the God who controls the outcome. It's not the same thing as optimism. Optimism is fickle, even if you're the treasured and sunny children's character Pollyanna. (Come to think of it, that was actually kind of the point of that whole story.) Everyone loses their rosy glow at some point. Faith is something else. Here's why you can continue when the world is less than wonderful and everything seems to be crumbling:

Because glass slippers shatter, but shoes of peace do not.

God gives us peace that passes understanding as our footwear, in His generosity and love. I cannot get over the fact that God cares enough to provide us with shoes.

"That's precious Melinda, but how does that relate back to Anastasia?"

First of all, everything in life basically relates back to Anastasia in one way or another. I once sat in Branson, Missouri and watched a musical adaptation of "It's a Wonderful Life" where George Bailey leaned over the bridge he had considered ending his life on and dramatically sang the lyrics

"Heart don't fail me now, courage don't desert me." If the plight of sainted Christmas character George Bailey can relate back to Anastasia anything can.

There's that scene at the end when she finally faces down Rasputin. He's led her out into an isolated garden thinking he will win this last battle with her. Unfortunately, the dark arts bargain he has made has him carrying around a vial connected to his life force.

"I'm not afraid of you," Anastacia declares.

"I can fix that," Rasputin snarls as he causes the foundation beneath her to crumble. This struggle takes several moments, but it culminates in the instant his vial is snatched from his hands and rolls down the precipice, straight under Anastasia's foot. She looks him straight in the eye, accentuating every stomp with her words.

"This is for Dimitri."

Stomp.

"This is for my family."

Stomp.

"And this is for you."

With one final stomp of her foot the vial shatters, destroying Rasputin at long last.

"DasviDAniya, Anya," indeed.

Your feet, they are powerful too.

It was Easter time at New Life St. Louis not too long ago and I was to write the Easter monologue. This happy task often falls to me and it happens to be one of my favorites. This year Shepherd was preaching on the topic "Game Over," and I was honestly baffled. How, how, HOW was I going to fit "Game over" into a spoken word that didn't reference Nintendo Switches or PS4's? The line I ended up crafting said:

> "No more living in lack, no more laden with fear, no more need to look over your shoulder. Hey Thomas! You can believe it or not, but I'm calling it. Game over."

It was still not my favorite line because I was still not super inspired by this sermon topic. (Let's not tell my pastor when we run into him, K? Okay.)

I honestly don't know what came over me when I was in the moment where it was actually time to deliver this word to the body. I yelled the line out with authority. I said:

"I am calling it now, IN JESUS NAME, game over" and I stomped my foot with authority when I did it. I felt the Holy Ghost in that moment in such a strong way. The feeling reverberated up from the sole of my foot to the top of my head like the waves of sound were tangible. Why?

> *"The God of peace will soon crush Satan under your feet. The grace of our Lord Jesus be with you,"*
>
> Romans 16:20

There is authority in your footwear. There is power in your feet. If your fairy tale has lost its luster, if your rose-colored glasses have been trampled, just know the God who formed you created you to take territory. Just like He promised Joshua, He will give you every place where you set your feet. (Joshua 1:3) You don't have to stay in defeat. You don't have to surrender to torment.

Put on your Princess shoes.

8

SPINNING STRAW TO GOLD, MULTIPLYING LOAVES

The story of Rumpelstiltskin has always intrigued me. The end of the story, involving the saving of a queen's first-born child and the guessing of the weirdest most impossible name imaginable is not what captivates my attention. It's the beginning of the tale that holds my thoughts. The Brothers Grimm told and preserved this story, of how a miller bragged far and wide he had a daughter that could spin straw into gold. The King, considering this a very useful skill to have, grabbed the girl and locked her in a room in a tower. The room was filled with straw. He demanded she spin that straw into gold by morning or she would lose her head. (It's worth pausing to note here that spinning wheels never seem to bring good luck or fortune in these stories, do they?) The girl is absolutely bewildered. She cannot turn straw into gold. She is literally incapable of doing that. A tiny impish man eventually appears out of nowhere, promising he will turn all the straw into gold in exchange for her necklace. The next day, the king is pleased with her progress and upgrades her to a bigger room filled with even more straw. She gets to spin that into gold over night or face the fate of losing her head. Luckily, the man returns and performs the task for her in exchange for her ring. The third night of this challenge is to be the last. If the girl settles into the room, now larger than ever before featuring the greatest quantity of straw yet, and spins it all into gold not only will she keep her head, but she will become a queen. If she fails, the king will look for a bride elsewhere as her head tumbles from her shoulders. How romantic. Thankfully, the tiny man shows up again to help her complete the task. There's just one problem: She has nothing left to trade. She barters with the life of her firstborn son, betting on something that doesn't exist yet to save her from her current state. That's not the part of the story I'm worried about today. You don't need to worry either, all of that works itself out in the end. What I'm captivated by is this situation, where she is given a task she cannot possibly complete on her own, and locked in a tower.

Have you ever felt like that? You know you are His, you know you are called, but the situation you find yourself in is just too much for you. You've been asked to do something and you just can't. You're not being a damsel in distress and you're not playing around, you literally just cannot do it.

If you have felt that way, you're not alone. I certainly have embodied those feelings. (I am the poster child for them even now as I sit in Arkansas with the clock running out, struggling to sort through all the words swirling in my head and get them on paper and out into the world). The disciples of Jesus had to feel that way too. They must have felt that way on more than one occasion, but this is the one instance that sticks out to me:

"When Jesus heard what had happened, he withdrew by boat privately to a solitary place. Hearing of this, the crowds followed him on foot from the towns. When Jesus landed and saw a large crowd, he had compassion on them and healed their sick. As evening approached, the disciples came to him and said,

This is a remote place, and it's already getting late. Send the crowds away, so they can go to the villages and buy themselves some food.' Jesus replied,

*'They do not need to go away. **You give them something to eat.'***

'We have here only five loaves of bread and two fish,' they answered.

'Bring them here to me,' he said. And he directed the people to sit down on the grass. Taking the five loaves and the two fish and looking up to heaven, he gave thanks and broke the loaves. Then he gave them to the disciples, and the disciples gave them to the people. They all ate and were satisfied, and the disciples picked up twelve basketfuls of broken pieces that were left over. The number of those who ate was about five thousand men, besides women and children,"

Matthew 14:13-21 (NIV)

None of the disciples had packed a lunch for 5,000 people that day and Jesus, cool, calm, and completely collected looked them in the face and said:

"You give them something to eat." He asked them to do something, knowing perfectly well there was no way they could accomplish the task set before them. It's not our skill set, our abilities, or our solutions that Jesus wants the most. What He requires, ultimately, is our obedience, no matter what. At the end of the day, that's what He's looking for. He's not worried about our supplies because His storehouse is limitless. He's not worried about our ability to perform because He is able to do anything. He just asks us to say "yes." Even when it seems impossible. Even when we can't do what He's asking on our own.

Sometimes I get up at five in the morning and you can find me sitting "criss-cross-applesauce" in the middle of my bed with prayer journals and inspirational books, my She Reads Truth Bible and notebooks all around me. I make tea. I play instrumental music. I even pray.

Sometimes I do that. And sometimes I teach 5th Grade.

Ha. ha. ha. What. Joy. It. is. to. laugh.

The other day I stumbled into the bathroom, turning the shower on with one hand and accessing my Bible app with the other. It was my hope that if I hit "play" and let whatever passage I am currently supposed to be reading filter through the shower steam I might somehow glean some knowledge from the Word by osmosis if nothing else.

My brain finally tuned in somewhere in the middle. Bible guy was reading about Gideon. I went from half asleep to whole awake in a matter of seconds. A story I had heard my whole life, a story I had read multiple times, spoke to me in a new way when I realized:

God comes to this man cowering in a wine press. He calls him "mighty warrior." He commands him to tear down his father's idols. He commissions him with the task of fighting in His name. He coddles him through a ridiculous series of fleeces and tests. I knew all that. I understood all that. That's not what got me. My ears zeroed in on the part where Gideon is told to start dismissing soldier after soldier from the army.

God adds a task beyond imagining to the "To Do" list. Then He immediately subtracts the resources with which to accomplish that task. God tells Gideon to triumph in battle, while simultaneously taking his tools.

When Gideon turns to God in bewilderment the Lord lets him know it's all good:

"With the three hundred men that lapped I will save you and give the Midianites into your hands. Tell everyone else to go home."

Could it be I think, not for the first time but not often enough, that it's not about me? That it's not about my resources? That when I look at what He wants me to do the tools don't matter as much as I think? What if I already have whatever I need to triumph? What if, whatever He's given me, that's what I need? What if I don't truly need anything more than everything I already have?

When He first finds Gideon, this is how the Angel of God addresses him. He calls him "Mighty Warrior." He tells him, this man who is the very least man of the very least family in the very least tribe in his nation:

"Go in the strength you have," (Judges 6:14). **Go in the strength you have.** I am shaken from head to knees.

"Am. I. Not. Sending. You?"

And I realize: You can come with your excuses. You can put out your fleeces. You can know all your weaknesses. But though your resources dwindle and your family is not prominent and your faith is not mighty you are His even so. And if He has sent you that is all you need to know. So go ahead Gideon. Go ahead and go.

You can go confidently into the place where He calls you right now, with the strength that you have, no matter how little that is.

You can do that because, it's not you who does the work. Is it?

> *"This can be nothing other than the sword of Gideon son of Joash, the Israelite. God has given the Midianites and the whole camp into his hands,"*

> Judges 7:14

Gideon wins the battle, because God always wins the battle.

You may not have much to offer. You may be worried about the meager resources or floundering faith or fleeting talents and skills but did you know a widow's mite is mighty in the hands of our great God?

"As Jesus looked up, he saw the rich putting their gifts into the temple treasury. He also saw a poor widow put in two very small copper coins.

'Truly I tell you,' he said, 'this poor widow has put in more than all the others. All these people gave their gifts out of their wealth; but she out of her poverty put in all she had to live on,'"

Luke 21:1-4 (NIV)

Let's go back to that passage where He feeds the five thousand so I can tell you what I love about it.

Jesus says:

"You give them something to eat." This is exactly what the disciples did. They gave the people something – not everything, because they didn't have that – and the Lord took that something and turned it into everything the crowd needed. He made something everything, with twelve baskets left over. How many disciples did he have? Twelve.

Twelve baskets left over. One to fill each disciple who had started with empty hands.

9

FULLY KNOWN AND
PERFECTLY PROTECTED

There are no words invented by human language capable of fully expressing the point enough:

There was absolutely no logical reason for the meltdown. I cannot make this any clearer, but I will try one more time for emphasis:

I melted down for no reason.

During the season of my life which forms the setting for the drama of this particular stage play, I was busy loving Jesus with my whole heart. I was also seeing a talented counselor for professional help. No worries, my counselor also loves Jesus with her whole heart. Here's how it started. I read a book called Afraid of all the Things. The more I read of the book, the more I identified with it. It was a book on anxiety and the author (Scarlet Hiltibidal) had a real knack for making you feel everything she was feeling. I mean, with each turn of page I identified so clearly with what she was saying. It was almost as if I were there. Almost as if I myself had lived some of this. The more I searched my memory, the more I realized, I had lived quite a bit of it. So what was going on? I finally called my sister, who also happens to be a licensed counselor, and I asked her:

"I don't know, I was just thinking, is it possible that I have this? That I might suffer from some anxiety?" She laughed. She laughed long. She laughed hard. She laughed enough that I briefly considered hanging up on her (a plan which would have had more follow through had I known this would be a story she would share in seminars). Apparently, it was very clear to her and many others who knew me that I suffered from anxiety but I genuinely did not know.

My sister and I were raised in a missionary home and the product of being reminded we were examples quite often and long trips to America for stints of fundraising. It's not that we were told or taught to be fake by any means, we just were never allowed to let our emotions dictate our behavior. We "pulled it together" and got through whatever we needed to get through no matter what. So that's how I lived my life. I thought everyone else was living this way as well. That everyone spent their teen years unable to sleep through a night, curled up outside their parent's bedroom door straining for the sounds of their breathing, just to make sure that was still happening. I thought every public speaker was violently physically ill before and after speaking. I was a grown woman who would get into her car and cry, thinking thoughts like:

"I bet Susan texted Sharon to meet her here before I got here so neither one of them would have to deal with me alone," about people who were my closest friends. I did, in fact, suffer from some anxiety, and at the time our story takes place I was actively receiving professional help.

It was an Instagram story that triggered it. I wish I could say there was anything remarkable about the Instagram story. I wish it had given me any sort of evidence that things were going south, that there was anything at all disturbing about the post in general. There wasn't. There really wasn't. And I quickly and effectively lost my mind anyway. I could not stop crying to save my own life.

It was around this time my mentor and friend Miriam

asked if I wanted to meet her at Target. I did desperately need to see her for help and comfort right at that moment, but I warned her I was not a pretty sight. Don't square your shoulders and start in with defensiveness towards the way I feel about myself, I am beautiful. I know. Thank you. I am not speaking from a place of low self-esteem. (Which is something I think we have already covered anyway). I am just trying to tell you realistically, I was not a pretty sight at this time. First of all, any sort of pretense my hair gives at even acting like it has the most miniscule amount of volume is accomplished by putting a lot of mousse in my very wet hair, scrunching it up to my scalp, and fastening it into place with six or seven colorful clips called "scrunch clips." I doubt that's what the salons call them, but I do believe it is their scientific name. This particular overnight hairstyle gives me some semblance of volume and body in the morning, but makes me look like I'm wearing a colorful football porcupine helmet of hair in the night. To add to this tragedy of fashion, I was already in my pajamas. I was weeping with too much force to change any of this, so I just threw a skirt on over said pajamas. In this alarming ensemble I poured myself like a waterfall of erratic emotion into my trusty Jeep named Jarvis, and I headed for Target.

As I sat in the car, vision becoming more tear-blurred by the mile, I thought to myself:

"Obviously, what my sister the licensed therapist and my actual licensed therapist would prefer I do is follow this situation through to the bitter end, mentally. I should think of the absolute worst that could happen and sit in it for a minute as I am driving, to try and discover what I would do in the event everything fell apart."

Both my sister and my therapist have since informed me this course of action is absolutely not at all what they would have preferred and would never recommend it – especially as I was already in a very precarious emotional state. Especially because I happened to be operating a motor vehicle at the time. They do not endorse this practice. They do not approve this message.

The further I drove, the harder it became to see, and the further I spiraled into my mental pit of despair:

"If this all falls apart I literally will not be able to live here. I will have to move. I cannot possibly stay here if this ends in ruin. I'll have to move to Europe. It will be fine. Deandra will take me. Matthew loves me. He will build me a grandmother suite attached to their beautiful house and they will have children and I will nanny and care for the children and write books and it will be fine. I'll just have to move to Europe."

I began mentally packing my bags and saying goodbye to each and every loved one in the town I had become so attached to. Each sorrowful face of each person I loved became more clear even as the road became more fuzzy. In this moment, I noticed something unfortunate.

Now, it's important to note:

My lips are never chapped. It's my spiritual gifting. Some people have the gift of prophecy, some serve or speak or sing or discern spirits. Me? My lips are never chapped. It's just the way it is. As a consequence of this happy gift from above, I do not own any chap stick. I simply never have it with me, because my lips are never chapped. Except for this night, of course, the night I am referencing. I began to notice my lips were chapped enough to feel like tiny forest fires on my face, and I had no sweet balm of chap stick to extinguish them. It was at this point I began to speak these words over and over again aloud:

"I am going to have to move to Europe and my lips are chapped and I don't have chap stick and I'm my going to have to move to Europe and I don't have chap stick and my lips are chapped." I am unsure why I felt speaking all of my misfortune out into the safe space of my empty vehicle would be helpful, but I put it to practice with a vengeance.

Just a reminder of how I looked:

Porcupine scrunch clips, pajamas, skirt over pajamas, chapped lips, bloodshot eyes, snot running. (Actual snot, actually running down my face, this is not something cute I'm just saying. Which, as if. Everyone knows snot is never cute.) Just a crazy woman attempting to drive as she screams about moving to Europe without chap stick at the top of her lungs.

Miriam had redirected course, so I turned the wheel of my vehicle toward Dairy Queen. Honestly it was a much more appropriate scene for the rest of my meltdown to play out. Target did not deserve to witness such a situation that night. Target is better than that.

When I pulled into the parking lot next to Miriam's car a couple of things happened.

First, Miriam realized there was no way on earth I needed to exit my vehicle to go into any sort of reputable dining establishment, including a Dairy Queen.

Secondly, I realized Miriam had her daughter with her. Her beautiful, perceptive, "can't pull one over on me even though I'm a child" daughter who never misses anything. Her creative daughter who had taken up video documenting with a vlog. Her daughter who definitely knew and was friends with students in my 5th grade class. Kylie and I made eye contact. (I think. I cannot possibly over-tell you how blurry everything was but then also sort of think you might be getting the picture by now. There are only so many times a person can type the word "blurry"). Instead of gracefully ignoring my fallen state, she got out of the car and came over to my window. Frantically wiping snot with one hand and slowly pushing the "down" button for my window with the other, I gave her a feeble smile and whispered,

"Hi. Watcha doing?" She smiled back, said,

"This is for you," and slipped a package of chap stick into my car with more skill and stealth than any drug dealer or pickpocket I've seen portrayed in plays or on film. I just stared at it a minute. Not calmly or peacefully of course, I definitely began crying harder.

"Thank you, Kylie." I choked out through sobs. "I really need this right now." She got back in her car, we rounded up, circled through the drive through, and headed for their house. I pulled into the driveway and waited for Miriam to get in the passenger's seat of my car with her ice-cream. We sat in silence for a minute as tears continued to roll down my face. I stared hard at the garage door of her home, finally slipping the chap stick over to her side of the car with a curt:

"Explain this please."

She said Kylie had been at the checkout when she grabbed the chap stick.

"What's that for?"

"Oh, this is for Mel."

"I don't know that Mel needs chap stick."

"I'm getting this for Mel."

"Kylie, IDK if you heard but Mel doesn't ever have chapped lips. It's her spiritual gifting. You can use your own money to get this, but I don't know that she'll want it." It was at this point in the conversation that Kyle squared her shoulders and announced with great determination,

"Melinda. Needs this chap stick. Right now." Miriam says she thought,

"Is there any way the Lord is telling my child Mel needs chap stick right now?"

That was, in fact, exactly what the Lord was doing.

How easily, when weighted down by the cares of life, I give myself over to editing Scripture. I remember to "seek first the kingdom," but I forget not to worry.

> *"Therefore I tell you, do not worry about your life, what you will eat or drink; or about your body, what you will wear. Is not life more than food, and the body more than clothes? Look at the birds of the air; they do not sow or reap or store away in barns, and yet your heavenly Father feeds them. Are you not much more valuable than they? Can any one of you by worrying add a single hour to your life? And why do you worry about clothes? See how the flowers of the field grow. They do not labor or spin. Yet I tell you that not even Solomon in all his splendor was dressed like one of these. If that is how God clothes the grass of the field, which is here today and tomorrow is thrown into the fire, will he not much more clothe you—you of little faith? So do not worry, saying, 'What shall we eat?' or 'What shall we drink?' or 'What shall we wear?' For the pagans run after all these things, and your heavenly Father knows that you need them. But seek first his kingdom and his righteousness, and all these things will be given to you as well,"*
> Matthew 6:25-33

I spend so much time agonizing over how things will work out or what's going to happen to me while I'm serving a God who cares enough to make sure I have chap stick when I need it. He's a God who has every little detail under control, because He cares about every detail. You are protected, no matter what.

> *"He will cover you with his feathers, and under his wings you will find refuge; his faithfulness will be your shield and rampart,"*
> Psalm 91:4

As a warrior in the fight, it is the most beautiful thing to know you can shelter under the wings of the almighty. His faithfulness also is your shield and your rampart.

Shield is a self-explanatory term, bringing a clear image to mind. It means exactly what it says, a shield like you have seen before, usually large and able to protect from all sorts of calamity.

Another word for "rampart" is "buckler." "Buckler" is Strong's concordance #5507 and "is defined as a feminine noun referring to a small shield, a buckler. It refers to a defensive weapon used to ward off the attacks and blows of an enemy. It is used figuratively of God's faithfulness to His people as their shield or protection."[2]

The faithfulness of God is our big shield and our little shield. In every way, we are covered and protected.

Psalm 84:11 is one of my favorite verses in the Bible.

> *"For the LORD God is a sun and shield; the LORD bestows favor and honor; no good thing does he withhold from those whose walk is blameless."*

The Lord is both a life-giving sun and sustenance to those who serve Him, and a shield of protection. You are fully known by your heavenly Father. He sees every need, feels every hurt, catches every tear. You are sheltered safe in His faithfulness, perfectly protected, shielded from harm, chap stick provided.

---

[2] Maryellenwrites.com

10

GIRL, GET YOUR TIARA

My sister and I grew up in Ghana, West Africa and one summer, during a return to the states, our parents sent us to youth camp. The camp we went to is well beloved in our movement, a beautiful camp full of excellence and hospitality, but I can honestly say I had close to the worst week of my entire life while there. It's just the way it went down. Our friends who begged us to go, found original, more cool friends they had known all their lives upon arrival. We weren't used to the food. We weren't used to the schedule. (We went to bed at 10:00 PM at the latest. Being locked out of our dorm rooms as a group till two in the morning was a foreign and horrifying concept to us.) Speaking of dorm rooms, my sister was the only person I really knew and we were separated by age into different rooms, as well as different groups throughout the day. The bathrooms were communal. Everyone thought I was a counselor as I roamed around alone. I don't know why, it was a really cool camp and absolutely none of the counselors were that frumpy. Man, was I frumpy. My go to outfit of choice at the time was a black jean skirt, which had been ripped. The rip had been repaired with a really cool fish patch. I loved the thing. No-one else had a fish patch on their skirt. How unique was that? We had also purchased, in bulk, a collection of faux turtle necks from Walmart. They were super comfortable, very American, and Christmas themed. Snow men, snowflakes, pine green, etc. It was my custom at the time to wear my hair slicked back in a greasy pony tail, which I would pull half way through so, a very slipper pony loop, if you will. Gorgeous. Dressed for success and struggling to fit in, I signed up to sing "Mary Did You Know" acapella in the talent show. You'll struggle to believe this but, that action did not gain me popularity.

At the end of the week I had a Scarlet O'Hara moment of great sincerity. I clutched the dirt of the campground in my fist, lifted it to the sky and declared

"As God is my witness, I will never return to this campground again." And I meant it.

Years later I said "yes" to speaking at a conference, a beautiful invitation that still humbles and honors me to this day. I didn't think to check where the conference was being held, and became immediately nauseous as I pulled up to the site of that awful week at camp.

I was older, I was wiser. I had long since gotten rid of the fish skirt, but I was still that same frightened, intimidated, awkward little girl inside. I couldn't get ahold of myself. I was physically ill any time I was on the premises. I laid out in my hotel room before time to speak, nose to floor. I will never forget when the Lord said to me:

"I allowed you to feel like nothing so you would know it is I alone who have made you everything you are. "The girl in the fish skirt had experienced a wardrobe change of more than one kind.

The Bible, it turns out, has some things to say about clothes:

> *"I counsel you to buy from me gold refined in the fire, so you can become rich; and white clothes to wear, so you can cover your shameful nakedness; and salve to put on your eyes, so you can see,"*

> Revelation 3:18

58

I read something like that and I'm thinking: "Wow. What kind of Existential Etsy Shop is this?" For some context, we look to the verses just before these.

> *"I know your deeds, that you are neither cold nor hot. I wish you were either one or the other! So, because you are lukewarm—neither hot nor cold—I am about to spit you out of my mouth. You say, 'I am rich; I have acquired wealth and do not need a thing.' But you do not realize that you are wretched, pitiful, poor, blind and naked,"*

Revelation 3:15-17

These words are being written to the church in Laodicea. The Laodiceans built an aqueduct to bring cold water down from the mountains. When it left the mountains, it was ice cold, but by the time it made that trip all the way down the mountains to Laodicea, it was lukewarm.

Now, down in the valley where the Lycus River joins the Maeander River, there were hot springs. However, when they would take this hot water up to Laodicea, by the time it got there, it was no longer hot — it had become lukewarm water.[3]

What He's talking about, when He talks to them about being hot or cold instead of lukewarm, is the importance of staying close to the source. And that's when he says:

> *"I counsel you to buy from me gold refined in the fire, so you can become rich; and white clothes to wear, so you can cover your shameful nakedness; and salve to put on your eyes, so you can see,"*

Revelation 3:18

From the time He clothes a disobedient Adam and Even in the garden, He is saying: I want you to get your clothes, your stuff, your importance, your identity from me. And when we look at the kind of clothes He wants to give us

---

[3] Laodicean Water by Peter Leithart from patheos.com

they are so. much. better. than anything we could purchase from anywhere else.

> *"Strength and honor are her clothing; She shall rejoice in time to come,"*

Proverbs 31:25

> *"Consider the lilies how they grow: they toil not, they spin not; and yet I say unto you, that Solomon in all his glory was not arrayed like one of these. If then God so clothe the grass, which is to day in the field, and tomorrow is cast into the oven; how much more will he clothe you, O ye of little faith? And seek not ye what ye shall eat, or what ye shall drink, neither be ye of doubtful mind. For all these things do the nations of the world seek after: and your Father knoweth that ye have need of these things. But rather seek ye the kingdom of God; and all these things shall be added unto you,"*

Luke 12:27-31

> *"I will rejoice greatly in the LORD, My soul will exult in my God; For He has clothed me with garments of salvation, He has wrapped me with a robe of righteousness, As a bridegroom decks himself with a garland, And as a bride adorns herself with her jewels,"*

Isaiah 61:10

And here's my favorite part of this whole clothes situation. David is talking about the Lord who…

> *"redeems your life from the pit and crowns you with love and compassion, who satisfies your desires with good things so that your youth is renewed like the eagle's,"*

Psalm 103:4-5

> *"Therefore you are no longer a slave, but a (and put the feminine word here) daughter; and if a daughter, then an heir through God,"*

Galatians 4:7

Charity Gayle's "In Jesus Name" begins to play through my head and I sing the words confidently and sweetly:

"Crushed the darkness, made a fool of death and grave, oh King Jesus - you make royals out of slaves."

I am like "YES. Tiara." This is all the evidence I need.

To highlight why wearing a tiara might be important, we turn to the story of the woman in Scripture who was most likely to have been wearing one. Queen Esther. You've heard the story, you know the drill. The king had been in search of a new wife and Esther's beauty and charm won out over everyone else in the kingdom. Then, a wicked petty man named Haman sought to destroy all the Jews because he was angry at one Jew in the city. Esther was called upon to intercede for her people because, and here is the secret nobody knew, she was also a Jew. Mordecai came to Esther for help, and here was her response:

> *"All the king's officials and the people of the royal provinces know that for any man or woman who approaches the king in the inner court without being summoned the king has but one law: that they be put to death unless the king extends the gold scepter to them and spares their lives. But thirty days have passed since I was called to go to the king."*

Esther 4:11

When Esther's words are reported to Mordecai he says

> *"For if you remain silent at this time, relief and deliverance for the Jews will arise from another place, but you and your father's family will perish. And who knows but that you have come to your royal position for such a time as this?"*

Esther 4:14

She says:

"Any man or woman who approaches the king in the inner court" and he reminds her "You are not just any woman."

I heard Raymond Woodward speak on this one time and he said the rule may have applied to her in broad general terms, but it was not written for her. It was written for any regular man or woman. She was not just any man or woman, she was a queen.

> *"On the third day Esther put on her royal robes and stood in the inner court of the palace, in front of the king's hall. The king was sitting on his royal throne in the hall, facing the entrance. When he saw Queen Esther standing in the court, he was pleased with her and held out to her the gold scepter that was in his hand. So Esther approached and touched the tip of the scepter."*

Esther 5:1-2

The King's immediate reaction to her presence is something like:

"See that one wearing the tiara? That's my queen. Get over here baby, what do you want? I'll divide my kingdom in half for you."

We read in the text the story of Haman going home and he's all puffed up about being invited for dinner but not one time does he say anything like:

"You will never guess what happened! The Queen had the NERVE to show up in court today!" And honestly I still remember from Sunday School this being a big dramatic deal.

"He extended the scepter to her." **Of course** He did. It was a royal court. She was a royal. She was the queen. She belonged there.

Bro. Woodward said the problem was, she was a queen, but she was still thinking like a slave. God had positioned her, and she needed to step up and own that position.

When I got up this morning and looked in the mirror you know what I saw with my natural eye? A teenage girl with slicked greasy hair wearing a faux turtle neck and a black "dressy" jean skirt with a fish patch on it. Sometimes you have to look in the mirror, insert yourself into Scripture, and speak the truth. Here's how I do that with Colossians 3:9-17:

> You, Melinda Poitras have taken off your old self with its practices and you have put on a new self which is being renewed in knowledge in the image of its Creator. Here there is no Gentile or Jew or circumcised or uncircumcised or barbarian or Scythian or slave or free but Christ is all and is in all. Therefore, you, Melinda Poitras, God's chosen are holy and dearly loved and you will clothe yourself with compassion, kindness, humility, gentleness and patience. You will bear with these women, you'll forgive anyone who hurts you just like Jesus did for you, and above everything else you will put on love which will bind everyone together in perfect unity. The peace of Christ will rule in your heart, as you are all members of one body called to peace. You will be thankful. The message of Christ will dwell among you as you Melinda Poitras admonish with wisdom through psalms, hymns, and songs from the Spirit, and maybe some interpretive dance if you feel inspired with gratitude in your heart. And whatever you do in word or deed you Melinda Poitras will do all in the name of the Lord Jesus, giving thanks to God the Father through Him. You are a princess. Put on your tiara and act like it.

You too are a princess. Go get your tiara and act like it.

I'll say it again. You are a Warrior Princesses clothed in strength, honor and the armor of God.

Put on your princess crown. Pick up your sword.

But remember who gave you that sword, remember whose authority you speak in, remember whose power you fight in - remember, at the end of the day, where crowns go.

"The twenty-four elders fall down before him who sits on the throne and worship him who lives for ever and ever. They lay their crowns before the throne and say: 'You are worthy, our Lord and God, to receive glory and honor and power, for you created all things, and by your will they were created and have their being."

Revelation 4:10-11

I didn't understand this until I saw Ben Wishaw portray King Richard from the play Richard II. In Act IV he abdicates the throne to Henry IV. He wrestles with himself with great force and conflict before finally collapsing to the floor and casting his precious crown across it to land at the new king's feet. It was a bloody moment and movement. It cost him something. It cost him everything. And that moment, it stayed in my head, because that's what Jesus wants from me.

Casting our crowns is not about merely tossing aside some sparkly hair accessory. Our hopes, our dreams, our possessions, our livelihoods, our very identity – that's what He means by crown. Everything we have, every tiny glittering glimpse of glory, He wants that. It's not just a beautiful gesture, it's a bloody business. It will cost me something. It will cost me everything.

For Him to be truly King I get no glitter or glory. It is bloody. It just is. This is the beauty though: when I push my crown into the palm of His hand I get the pleasure of His presence as a present. When I truly take off my crown, only then can I put on the full person of Christ. Anything it costs me is nothing compared to everything I gain.

"Ay, and no, no and ay, for I must nothing be; therefore no no, for I resign to thee."

You are needed. By your family, your coworkers, your friends, the people you pass in the street today. There is only one beautiful you in this wide, wonderful world and when you own that, when you really own your identity in

Him? It changes everything, especially the people around you.

Put on your princess crown. Pick up your sword. Remember who you fight for. Remember where crowns go. Go ahead and take territory in the name of Jesus.

11

PRESERVED BY DISASTER

I once shelled out the extra cash to gain admittance to the St. Louis Science Center's exhibition of Pompeii. It was an incredible experience, well worth the money, and I was amazed as I wandered through the replica of what homes would have looked like during 79 A.D., gazing upon actual utensils, pots, and bowls which had been used during the time. I watched videos reenacting what it must have looked like when the volcano erupted, and ash began to flood down into the village area. I heard fake screams, imagined the real heart attack, and looked at whole life-size casts of the people found in the ruins. While we were enjoying a meal afterward my mind wandered back to the plates and bowls we had seen in the exhibit. I threw down my fork with dramatic force and exclaimed to my friend,

"I bet the ash from the volcano preserved the utensils! Those things we saw behind the glass were probably the actual. Bowls. And plates. From the actual Pompeii!" My friend stared at me blankly. Clearly she did not understand the depth of the revelation I had been given.

"Kristen!" I continued, "what I'm saying is that I think what we just saw in the museum were the actual artifacts from the actual Pompeii!" Kristen still seemed underwhelmed but, as it turned out I was just misreading her expression. It wasn't a lack of care or investment in the topic at hand, it was concern. Yes. Those were definitely the artifacts from the original Pompeii. When the volcano Mount Vesuvius erupted in 79 AD, sending nineteen feet or more of volcanic ash and debris hurtling toward the city of Pompeii, its "quick burial preserved it for centuries." The ruins were not found until the 16th century. Everything I had seen in the museum that day had been preserved by disaster.[4]

I was correct in my assessment, Kristen was not questioning that. She was just baffled that I had spent hours wandering through an exhibit that repeatedly told us that precise information, while actively missing the entire point. (Don't worry, this was long before I began my career as a teacher. The 5th graders of St. Louis were safe. At the time.)

Here's the good news I have for you; whether your life is at "My car wouldn't start this morning and I was late for work" or "Mt. Vesuvius is erupting and there is no way I will get out of the path of the volcanic ash in time" status. God is for you, He is with you, and your disaster is preserving you. And not in a "Your personal belongings and the cast of your body will end up in a museum full of ruins" sort of way.

> *"And we know that in all things God works for the good of those who love him, who have been called according to his purpose,"*
>
> Romans 8:28

The Lord is able to work good out of any material. I don't mean to sound like a preacher stuck on a verse, but if that helps it stick into your head then we'll go that route:

"Mhmm. That's good. Let me say it again. You go ahead and read it again. The Lord is able to work good out of any material. Any. Material. Whatsoever."

---

[4] Britannica.com

The fire, the illness, the abuse, the rape, the loss of a loved one, the unemployment, the childlessness – whatever it is, He is able to work good out of it whenever He wants to. He is able, and He will.

I was recently privileged to work on a book with missionary Lynne Jewett. The book is called Disasters Minister and it is to date my favorite thing I've ever done or worked on as far as writing goes. Justin Gleason interviewed me for his podcast, mentioned the book, and had a question for me regarding the title:

"When I see the word 'minister' I think of a lot of things. I think of faith. I think of the story you just told of miracles. I think of hope. I think of love. I think of spiritual gifts. The word that doesn't come to my mind, to be honest with you, is disaster. But you bring disaster into the idea as a power in this book, speak to us a little bit about that."

I explained a little bit about Lynne as a person and my involvement in the project before answering:

"She could look at her own life and view herself as a walking disaster. But the best part of it is the Lord meets her in every single part of the story, He comes through with the miraculous and then He uses her experiences to change someone else's."

> I referenced the Scripture about the God "who comforts us in all our troubles, so that we can comfort those in any trouble with the comfort we ourselves receive from God,"
>
> 2 Corinthians 1:4 (NIV)

"When she says 'disasters minister' it's just a reference to the way the Lord worked every part of her story for His glory and has used her life to minister to others."

I won't give spoiler alerts in this book because I would hate to rob you from running to read that one, but Lynne experiences disaster after disaster throughout the course of the story we tell in its pages, and the Lord worked every situation for His glory and her good. That's what He does. That's just what He does.

Bathsheba gets a pretty bad rap, if we're being honest. She's the cheating wife who was bathing lasciviously on her rooftop to many. Of course, in her defense, that was a common practice during those times and King David (who should have been on the battlefield, but instead was wandering around bored on his balcony) might have been less of a peeping Tom. He definitely could have been less of a domineering tyrant, bent on having his way, and not caring who he killed to get it, but this same David was a man after God's own heart if ever we've heard of one. (Talk about the Lord turning any situation around for His good.)

Bathsheba, she lost the baby that came out of that unfortunate bath time debacle. She was separated from her husband, carrying the guilt of his death around with her as she mourned the loss of a child and attempted to adjust to an entirely different life than she was accustomed to. Yet, the lord stepped into the midst of that disaster and showed Himself to be a redeemer, giving Bathsheba a place in the genealogy, the royal line of blood which would eventually produce the Christ.

He can use anyone, to do anything, at any time. There is nothing my God cannot redeem, restore, renew or re-establish. Whatever your situation is, He is able to work in the midst of it.

I have let go of things I never wanted to lose, I have said goodbye to things I thought I would keep forever, I have recovered from abuse, made wrong turns, melted down in parking lots. I have failed Him time and time again, but He has never once failed me. Looking back I always see, in the quiet corners I didn't notice, the crying nights I couldn't combat, and the lowest of the low, He was working for my good as even disaster preserved me.

12

SWORDS AND SOARING

"This is a cover crop." The Lord spoke this to me as I wrote in my journal in Apopka, Florida. I was praying about a relationship I was in at the time when those words rang through as clear as crystal and as loud as a bell.

"This is a cover crop." I had no recollection of ever hearing that phrase before, and I did not know what it meant. I went to the source of all knowledge – Google – to find the definition of this intriguing new concept. A cover crop is when you take care of crops for an entire year. You plant, you water, you cultivate, you shower them with love and attention, and then when it is time for harvest, you set those same crops you have lovingly tended on fire. You set the crop you've worked so hard to raise and grow on fire, for the good of the soil, and for the benefit of future, more integral crops.

My heart was broken. I knew exactly what this meant. This relationship I loved and delighted in cultivating was not meant for me to keep, it would not last forever, soon it would end, for the greater good of the soil.

Do you ever consider relocating your farm straight off His kingdom? I'm just asking for a friend. A friend who was genuinely considering such a thing on that day. What a time in the altar. Speaking of times in the altar, another one sticks out in my memory. To say I had been beaten down by life would have been a severe understatement. The Word of the Lord came to me in the form of a familiar voice that said "You have to get back up. You are tired and weary, battered and bruised, but you have to get back up. Clothe yourself in the strength of the Lord, pick up your sword, and fight."

Princesses know about ashes, don't they? Especially that one, named after the cinders. Cinderella was trapped in a home that harbored no comfort for her. Her father had died, leaving her with a brutal step-mother and two selfish step-sisters who did nothing but use, abuse, and berate her all day long. The work never ran out and the horrific barrage of cutting words never stopped coming. She was under fire day and night, and she slept as close to it at night as possible, desperately seeking some sort of warmth or comfort. As a consequence of this, she was always covered with ashes when she woke up in the morning. There are things I admire about Cinderella, a girl so acquainted with ashes her very name comes from them. I notice how she submitted to her season. I can see how her character was formed in the dark. She doesn't stay in the ashes though. She eventually gets up, cleans herself off, and makes it to a ball that changes her entire situation. She emerges beautiful, magical, glowing, pristine – just like a Phoenix from the ashes.

If you don't know, a Phoenix is a bird from ancient Greek mythology. Herodotus first made this legend popular. He told of a bird who would live for crazy extended periods of time (stretches of up to five hundred years) then die upon a self-constructed funeral pyre. When all hope seemed lost the Phoenix would regenerate itself, rising from the ashes. "To rise like a phoenix from the ashes means to emerge from a catastrophe stronger, smarter and more powerful."[5]

Okay Phoenix. It's your turn to rise. I don't know what life

[5] Grammarist

has thrown at you, I don't know what spirits have come against you, I don't know what loss you've endured or what loved ones have left, but I do know you have to get back up. You may be tired, weary, battered and bruised but you have to get back up. You clothe yourself in the strength of the Lord, you pick up your sword, and you fight. You pick up your sword and you fight right. Now.

I have not read one word of, or even seen one episode of Game of Thrones. (This is not a blanket statement of judgement over content, this is just a truth of my personal life I am attempting to make clear.) I do think often though, about people's fascination with this show. I don't think it's the graphic sexual content, people can get that anywhere, and despite the admonition "sex sells," I don't actually think that's why people are watching, or not watching, shows. I think it has much more to do with the fact that we are made to wrestle with our enemies, to conquer kingdoms, to take territory, to fight and to win.

> *"Through faith they conquered kingdoms, administered justice, and gained what was promised,"*
>
> Hebrews 11:33

We are warriors, created in His image, born to seize, claim, and defend territory for His kingdom. We are meant to pick up our swords.

I knew this, and the Lord was developing this message within me, a message about princesses and swords. I wanted a visual, so I went on Amazon and having done 0.00 research about swords in general, especially the one I picked, I purchased a plastic sword. It arrived in a fairly unobtrusive box in the mail. I was dubious at best, laughing at my own inability to read about dimensions or measurements. This sword would be a dud and that served me right.

When I opened the box, it turned out to be a very thick, durable, plastic that clicked together in three separate parts to form a sword almost as tall as I was. This was some heavy-duty, pretty impressive, Lord of the Rings type mess. I set to work jousting invisible foes in the kitchen immediately. I Marco Polo'ed my friends to show off this monstrosity and waved it around in a manner which made them very glad it was only plastic. There was no way around it. Amazon was winning. I was impressed.

I got in the car and went to meet up with my pastor's wife for lunch and I was just chattering away to the Lord:

"Wow this thing shows up and it's kind of weaponlike, I mean, it's HUGE. I am just so shocked by this, I don't even know...," and the Lord says:

"This is representing your Sword of the Spirit, so what did you expect it to look like?" And I immediately started bawling. I don't know why I expected it to be puny. I don't know why I thought it would look insignificant.

> *"For the weapons of our warfare are not carnal, but mighty through God to the pulling down of strong holds; Casting down imaginations, and every high thing that exalteth itself against the knowledge of God, and bringing into captivity every thought to the obedience of Christ,"*
>
> 2 Corinthians 10:4-5

The Lord has placed His word, the sword of the Spirit, into the hands of you, yes you. Sitting on the couch or laying on the beach or holding this book with one hand as you wipe down your countertops with the other – you, woman and warrior, have been given the Sword of the Spirit. It is a weapon for you to pick up and brandish and fight with and say:

"Sickness, you don't get to torture my mama. Porn, you don't get to have my son. Adultery, you take your hands off my husband. Not today Satan! You do not get to discourage my pastor, you do not get to lie to my friends about their sexuality, you do not get to trap my youth group in depression and anxiety - I come against you in the name of Jesus. I. Said. Not. Today."

There was one speaking engagement which opened the door to the rest of them. Looking back, I know this. One, right at the very beginning. I was deep in the thick of preparation for it. I hadn't been doing ladies events very long, so I was very new to all of it. Speaking in general has never been a goal of mine, just something the Lord ordains and allows on occasion. During the week leading up to the event I opened my eyes in the night and saw a dark being, like a cloud of mist or smoke, hurtling towards me. No sooner had I startled awake than I opened my mouth and a sword flew out of it. The sword collided with the cloud and when it did, every bit of the mist and smoke evaporated, the enemy was quickly and immediately vanquished.

> *"He made my mouth like a sharpened sword, in the shadow of his hand he hid me; he made me into a polished arrow and concealed me in his quiver,"*

Isaiah 49:2

The first time I pulled out that sword and spoke the full message the Lord had laid on my heart, women went crazy. I cannot even tell you the feeling of life and strength and empowerment that filled the entire room. The Holy Spirit did such a work. I watched God raise up an army.

Recently, I spoke somewhere and was forced to cut what I meant to be a very well-crafted, moving and funny message in half. I didn't get to speak the princess parts, I only spoke about the sword. So many women came up to me afterwards saying the same thing: We know we're princesses. We desperately needed to hear we are warriors as well.

Girls. I gotchu.

You, you reading this book right now, are equipped to

combat whatever dark force of the spirit, real world calamity, or impossible ill that comes against your peace, your family, your community, your church, your finances – the list goes on and on. Whatever the Lord has given you, He has also given you the ability to protect and defend. He has given you a weapon. He has made you into a weapon. You thought disaster would overtake you, you thought despair would consume you but He has plans for your life beyond imagining and you are needed. Your friends need you. Your family needs you. Your church and your community need you.

Get up. Pick up your sword. Fight. You are a woman and a warrior full capable of conquering kingdoms, gaining justice, and obtaining all that has been promised to you. Hold on to that sword and just like a phoenix rising from the ashes, you soar girl, soar.

13

PRODIGALS, PARTIES AND PREPARING A TABLE

When I come alive in my very first memory, I am standing in a kitchen in Nigeria. I remember distinctly how the concrete feels beneath my feet, the cooking smells mixing with the heavy humidity in the air as rain pelts the tin roof relentlessly. There's a commotion going on. People are crowding at the doorway to the outside world, laughter is breaking out in spurts of giddy delight, and my mother is singing.

> "Raindrops keep falling on my head, and
> just like the guy whose feet are too big for his bed,
> nothing seems to fit, oh
> raindrops keep falling on my head, they keep falling."[6]

Investigating what has caused this explosion of joy, I push through the crowd to spot my baby sister, toddling around with her umbrella, splashing in puddles and giggling with glee.

My second ever memory is the intense heat of betrayal. I was not allowed to play in the rain. I, with free spirit and winsome wandering stitched into the very fabric of my soul was denied every attempt at the rain frolic which so appealed to me. My sister did it, and it was a noteworthy

---

[6] Raindrops Keep Falling On My Head song by B. J. Thomas

event, worthy of celebration and recording for posterity.

My third ever memory is jealousy. I had experienced anger; that was cruel. I had experienced fury; that was overwhelming. But I had yet to experience jealousy. And jealousy? You cannot stand with that. That's the thing which will cripple you.

> *"Anger is cruel and fury is overwhelming, but who can stand before jealousy?"*
>
> Proverbs 27:4

We have some good parents. They nipped the jealousy thing in the bud with intention. (Thank God. The child has an accomplishment list longer than the road from our gate to our favorite childhood chop bar.) One of the sneaky parenting tools they used was giving me a birthday gift each time we celebrated her birth so I knew I too was special and loved. Here's the thing about that though:

Eventually they stopped doing it. They stopped because I was old enough to know: **This might be her birthday but my birthday is coming**. It's okay that she gets presents now. I'll get presents later.

The Sunday after her engagement, people at our church came up to me, and they hugged me, and they told me "congratulations." I loved this. Not just because it's a beautiful picture of how I feel about my sister and the way they all know it, but because that is how it should be.

We are a body. One body. A win for one is a win for all of us. My feet are sitting here with me right now, and they are not jealous that my hands are typing. They know their place, they know the places they get to take me, and they know I'm far more likely to get a pedicure than a manicure when the time comes anyway. A win is a win! Period.

Somebody gets assigned a solo? Congratulations to me.

Somebody gets a job promotion? Congratulations to me.

Somebody is pregnant? Congratulations to me.

It's the body. Healthy is healthy. When God blesses others, I should be just as grateful for that as if He were blessing me.

And here's the thing about rain y'all:

IT GETS ON EVERYONE.

I just wanted that to be extra noticeable because I think it's extra noteworthy. An open heaven is an open heaven. I'm serious, have you seen the way rain works? Ready or not. Just or unjust. When rain falls, it's falling on us all.

There's another verse to the song my mother is singing in my memory:

> "Raindrops keep falling on my head, but
> that doesn't mean my eyes will soon be turning red,
> crying's not for me, oh
> I'm never gonna stop the rain by complaining."

That's a beautiful sentiment about the futility of complaint in an unfortunate season of life, but that last line is not entirely true. Life and death are in the power of your tongue, and you actually can stop the rain of God's blessing in your life by complaining.

> *"From the fruit of their mouth a person's stomach is filled; with the harvest of their lips they are satisfied. The tongue has the power of life and death, and those who love it will eat its fruit,"*
> Proverbs 18:20-21

What if all you had to eat today was the "fruit of your mouth?" (The things you've said about other people, the way you've spoken to or about yourself, the response you've given when met with something or someone unpleasant.) Would you be filled and satisfied, or would you contract a case of food poisoning? Would your storehouse be full of harvest or barren and dry?

I won't soon forget the day I collapsed into the chairs of the chapel at Indiana Bible College, absolutely wrecked by the news of the success of someone who had wronged me. I didn't mean it maliciously, I didn't mean to be cruel, or hateful, or rebellious, I just spoke the truth from my wounded, injured spirit:

"This is not preparing a table before me in the presence of my enemies." It felt like a fancy dinner table had been laid and those who had wronged me were the only guests being invited.

The children of Israel had a similar query when they were traveling in the desert. Deliverance did not look like they expected, and dinner definitely wasn't tasting like they would have wanted it to. They said:

"Can God really spread a table in the wilderness?"
Psalm 78:19 (NIV)

What a question coming from the same lips that ate manna, but I can relate. How easily I become disgruntled with my place in His kingdom – especially when I have the status of others to compare it to.

There's a well-known story of a son who squanders his father's inheritance. Taking his share of the family holdings early, he runs off to enjoy his days with riotous living and wasteful abandon. His funds run out and without money to entice them his friends soon follow suit, abandoning him entirely. He is left with no other option than to care for, eat by, and sleep with the pigs. From his lowly state he realizes, things were better for even the servants in his father's house. He purposes in his heart to return home, not knowing what welcome he might receive.

We are all familiar with the story found in Luke chapter fifteen. The father he used, abandoned, and treated so poorly waits every day at the end of the road, longing to witness his safe return. When he spots his son coming down the road he begins to run toward him, welcoming him back with open arms and rejoicing. A robe is called for, the fatted calf is slaughtered, the wayward son has come home. There is someone, however, who is less than enthused with the prospect of this party:

> *"Meanwhile, the older son was in the field. When he came near the house, he heard music and dancing. So he called one of the servants and asked him what was going on.*
>
> *'Your brother has come,' he replied, 'and your father has killed the fattened calf because he has him back safe and sound.' The older brother became angry and refused to go in. So his father went out and pleaded with him. But he answered his father,*
>
> *'Look! All these years I've been slaving for you and never disobeyed your orders. Yet you never gave me even a young goat so I could celebrate with my friends. But when this son of yours who has squandered your property with prostitutes comes home, you kill the fattened calf for him!'*
>
> *'My son,' the father said, 'you are always with me, and everything I have is yours. But we had to celebrate and be glad, because this brother of yours was dead and is alive again; he was lost and is found,'"*

Luke 15:25-32

The prodigal son was lost in the world, and upon his return home we find his older brother, in my opinion a little lost too. He was so concerned about what his brother was getting, he forgot about what he had. Everything his father owned was also his inheritance but he failed to rejoice in the beauty of it, choosing instead to bear the weight of all he was begrudging.

2 Samuel chapter nine tells the story of Mephibosheth. He was the son of Jonathan, friend of David. His nurse was fleeing to safety while cradling him in her arms during battle, and she dropped him, leaving him crippled. Years later when he was fully grown, King David sent for him,

not to destroy what was remaining of a rival house but to invite him, this ruined, crippled, prince who had no fortune or title to speak of, to eat at his table every day. He didn't deserve it. He didn't earn it, but he "ate at the kings table continually, though he was lame in both feet," (2 Samuel 9:13).

On my worst day, when I have done nothing to contribute to the meal and am undeserving, when my name is not prominent and my soul is weary and my feet have been crippled by jealousy, the Lord is, in fact, able to spread a table right in the wilderness. He is able to, and He does.

"Trust in the Lord and do good: Dwell in the land, and feed on His faithfulness. Delight yourself also in the Lord, and He shall give you the desires of your heart. Commit your way to the Lord, trust also in Him, and He shall bring it to pass,"
Psalm 37:3-4 (NKJV)

When the desires of your heart seem out of reach remember your task is simple: Dwell in the land. Feed on His faithfulness. Delight yourself in Him. He is the one who gives the desires of our hearts. He is the one who brings the work to pass.

He sets a table in the wilderness, just for you. It is custom made, full of goodness, and the perfect opportunity to feed on His faithfulness, every single day.

May we react to blessing with the understanding we are all one body.

May we understand that true gratitude for blessing - even blessing given to others - is a trademark of Christian love.

May we be the happiest, most charming guest at any party - birthday, bridal, or baby.

May our words taste like cake as we attend the special occasion of our one life with our sisters and friends, celebrating all of God's good gifts given, together.

14

WHISTLE WHILE YOU GROW WEARY

Snow White is the most annoying of all the Disney Princesses. I'm sorry, I said what I said and I'll stand by it till the death. She is always singing in her shrill little voice, optimistic even though she has absolutely no reason to be, running around with her animals weirdly, and I am sorry. Okay. I'm sorry, but I just have to put this out there:

NO-ONE IS THAT HAPPY TO BE CLEANING!

Yes, I really feel that last sentence more than warranted the usage of all caps. Plus, I'm probably just a little bitter that I can't whistle.

Speaking of cleaning, I wish that weren't a big part of what love does. I wish church toilets could scrub themselves and the homeless and hungry had homes, and weren't hungry, and that my own home and personal space didn't look quite so much like it was inhabited by a hapless, hopeless hobo. (I am the hobo. The hobo is me.)

I have more than one friend who is brilliant. But I have only one who writes me personal e-mails like this:

> "The more I read through the Bible, the less I see of starry-eyed idealism and blissful youthful hope. I think of how the walls of the palace must have darkened the stars in Esther's eyes; how the sun in the

83

> hot fields scorched Ruth's idealism; and the weary endless days simply killed hope. Nothing to look forward to, nothing to hold on to, except for the promise of Love. Yet, behold, in time, a queen and a bride. And I think, was it because they staked so much - youth, hope, dreams - on the faithfulness of Love that - in utter surrender to that Love - they found their story?"

This same friend of mine sat next to me on a couch in Africa and confided how she's been meaning to write about the fact that love packs suitcases.

"Love packs suitcases, Melinda. Love does laundry." Then later someone speaks to me about Elisabeth Elliot and how when her husband was dead and her future seemed bleak she always committed to doing the very next thing. Whatever He wanted her to do. Whatever it was. One step at a time. Even if the "next thing" was the laundry.

Here are some things I have learned recently:

- I have learned that happiness is not a person.

- I have learned relationships are temporary but the things you invest in the soul of a person are not.

- I have learned blessings can come in some pretty interesting disguises.

- I have learned that it's not about me being "okay" - it's about me being better. And that sometimes, "better" hurts.

- I have learned that we don't always get what we deserve. We don't get all of the good things we DO deserve now, so that we might get all of the eternal things we DON'T deserve later.

- I have learned that they call it "peace that passes understanding" because sometimes you're in a good mood when you really shouldn't be.

- I have learned that so much in life, is perspective.
- I have learned to do the "next thing."

When I moved to Bloomington, Indiana briefly in an attempt to make a long standing career out of diapering children that aren't mine and start building a couple of other things that aren't mine either this same friend said to me:

"I want you to be happy too. I want you to be blessed."

And I replied, that so much of life is the grace of God. And that if we don't think I will inevitably be just as blessed to stand beside that white dress as she is to wear it - we are looking at blessings wrong.

I'm learning to **mean** *that.* Because above all else, I have learned that true love isn't all wax-sealed envelopes and red roses. Sometimes, it isn't *any* wax-sealed envelopes and red roses. (Unless, of course, these things are being delivered to the person next to you). Love. What can I say? Love does laundry. Love packs luggage. Love lurks in dark corners just as often as it ever frolics in sunshine. And in these moments of struggle, in these crazy days of blessing, in these times when I work in the infant room and sometimes (I'm not even ashamed to admit this) cry harder than they do - I learn to love. I learn to love with insane and inconceivable, ridiculous, unadulterated, wild abandon - **because I learn who Love is**.

A lesson in love. I begin to feel that is all this book is. All each day is. All my life is meant to be comprised of. Loving right and loving well - that's the majority of what matters.

I love that Amy Carmichael.

"People who worked closely with Amy Carmichael found it nearly impossible, after her death, to think of any faults. Perhaps memory did its beneficient work of erasure. One man, however, after weeks of thought, volunteered that Amma[7] indeed had at least one weakness: Sometimes she misjudged folk. When asked in what way, he said, 'She thought they were better than they were.'"

All Amy did her whole beautiful life was love people. That was all really. It was in every single line of every single book she wrote and every letter of each word I've read about her. The whole of her life was a dedication to love - first Jesus - then others. The two go hand-in-hand. She had no patience for those who failed to understand so simple and obvious a concept.

Her life was full of love and consequently, positively *teeming* with pain. "I am at an end, I do not understand, I fear I have not strength to go on" **pain**. I guarantee you - **where love is deep, pain cuts deeper**.

This does not, as a rule, seem fair but that's the thing:

When you insist upon seeing others as they could be - you still have to love them as they are.

Ann Voskamp says that "Love will always cost you grief, but love is always worth the price."

This is disjointed. I know. It doesn't live up to my usual fluidity (or the fluidity I imagine that I have in my brain). I know. But that's part of the lesson. Life gets choppy and love gets dicey: Cry. Crash. Cope. Repeat. Pray. Pray. Pray. That's how it can look. What do you do? Love. Anyway. Why? I'll tell you why *I* do:

Because Someone loved me. When I was worthless and hopeless and in general less than I should be. (So... This morning). When I was broken and breaking everything

---

[7] Amma means « mother » and was a title given Amy while in India, https://www.bu.edu/missiology/missionary-biography/c-d/carmichael-amy-beatrice-1867-1951/ accessed May 12, 2022

that I touched as a result. When I had lost my way and was losing my mind. When I did all within my power to make Him sorry - *He wasn't sorry*. When I wasn't even worth it anymore - *I was worth it to Him*. "By one who loves is another kindled" and He has set me on fire, and if I do not **love** I do not **love Him,** and I **will** love Him until I die or **I will die trying**.

As foolish as it may seem in all your worn out and your weary, and yes, probably your laundry, this is my recommendation: Cry. Crash. Cope. **And hope**.

Love is a force of nature unending because *when you are swimming in a sea of grace, the grace to be gracious never runs out.* This is truly inconceivable (I know - I looked it up, so I do know what that word means. PS: If you get the reference award yourself unlimited gold stars) but there it is.

> "This is how your broken, dismembered heart is re-membered - when you remember to count the ways He loves."
>
> Ann Voskamp

Remember my brilliant friend from a little earlier in the chapter? The one who writes the incredible emails? Here's another taste of their writing.

> "What if Love stories were for sale, in the section of heaven where destinies are given out? What if they cost all our starry-eyed ideals, and youthful hope, and blissful ignorance and dreams of sunshine? What if they simply required us to walk straight into the ugly of life with eyes wide open and experience it? For the Love is there. I cannot argue with this. My heart knows it, no matter what is happening. The Love is there. But the story must be written by me and you. Am I willing to press on, to enter the jungle of next steps, and school and begin the next chapter in my story? To lose what little of my hope or blissful

> optimism remains? And yet to find, round every corner and next to every painful event, that the Love is there. The Love is there. The Love is there. Am I willing to walk through my story, so that Love may meet me in it?"

Every single day - happy, sad, glad, mad, or a mixture of all of the above - Love steps out to meet me in my story. So I am happy. So I am blessed. Especially on the days that I get to do the laundry.

I'm also weary a lot of the time. Just to be honest, just to put it out there, attempting to love Him and love others and do both of those things well flat out wears me out at times. I do attempt to cultivate all the attributes of a Proverbs 31 woman. I do! But who could possibly measure up to that? First of all, the Bible literally says:

"She grabs the spindle with her fingers," which would have been a skill I think we can all agree Sleeping Beauty could have practiced more efficiently. It's just a lot. In order to encapsulate her character I would have to be both worth more than rubies and hard to find. (When the day comes that my self-esteem is at 'precious gem' status I don't know that we should assume I'll be hiding that sparkling light under a bushel). I would love for my husband to have full confidence in me and fully intend to bring him good and not harm all the days of his life but also – where is he? Talk about hard to find… I just don't know how I would do with selecting wool and flax, and though I work, I don't know that my hands are eager to do so. It's hard to rise in the night, even while providing food for my family. I consider fields but don't really have the wherewithal to buy them. Is my trading profitable? I am definitely not sleeping with a light on. (Although, I think that "her lamp does not go out at night" reference might be to burning the midnight oil and not sleeping at all). I would not fare any better with needles than Sleeping

Beauty did. I do open my arms to the poor but I don't always know what to do with them. I grew up in Africa, I actually am a little afraid of snow. If I tried to make a comforter for my bed or a rug for my living room it would end up as a rag for the dusting for sure. The same would definitely go for any linen garments I might make to sell. I don't foresee my Etsy shop really taking off into a success story just honestly. As long as we're being honest at this level, the whole thing kind of seems out of reach to me. I feel much more confident in my ability to embody the Scripture Proverbs 30:1 which reads:

"I am weary God, but I can prevail."

Here's the thing: I am weary at times, yes. But I can, in fact, prevail. I can, and so can you. Here's how I know:

> *"Let us not become weary in doing good, for at the proper time we will reap a harvest if we do not give up,"*
>
> Galatians 6:9 (NIV)

No matter where you are in life, there are some parts of Proverbs 31 you can embody no matter your productivity or energy level, absolute success guaranteed.

> *"She is clothed with strength and dignity; she can laugh at the days to come."*
>
> Proverbs 31:25 (NIV)

You can laugh at the future that's for you, no matter what season you're in, because you will reap a harvest if you do not give up.

> *"Charm is deceptive, and beauty is fleeting; but a woman who fears the Lord is to be praised,"*
>
> Proverbs 31:25

Cry. Crash. Cope. Hope. And go ahead and whistle while you grow weary. You will reap your harvest in the proper time, guaranteed. Fear Him. Trust Him. You are all you need to be, when He is all you need.

15

OF PRINCE ERIC
AND PRISONER BARABBAS

It was a coloring page that really did me in. I was sitting in South Dakota, coloring a picture of my favorite Disney Prince, which is of course, Prince Eric.

I cannot fathom I need to explain to you why I love Prince Eric, but in case I do let me give you some reasons:

- Dark full hair
- Ocean blue eyes
- Musical bent
- Lyrical laugh
- Love of dogs
- Boats

Honestly, do I even need to say more? As I was coloring my mind was wandering throughout the course of the whole story when I screamed for my friend Lanae to come into the room.

"This! This is what's wrong, right here! I have a Prince Eric complex!" She was laughing so hard she could no longer stand because my face was apparently the picture of sincere intensity. (Imagine that). Let's go into the story a little bit, shall we?

Ariel is a mermaid. Eric is a prince who loves the ocean. It happens that one of his nights of reel-dancing and flute-playing on his boat is interrupted by a storm which tosses him overboard. Ariel rescues him, singing all the while. When Eric comes to, all he remembers is her voice, whereas Ariel for her part, has committed every single second of this encounter to memory. The girl may be combing her hair with a fork, but she has every aspect of this relationship planned out. She is hooked – line and sinker. *(Please laugh at my punny fishing joke. No. Go ahead. Feel obligated. Do it to be polite if you have to! I insist).*

She is desperate to be with this man. So she turns to a sea witch, Ursula, to help her accomplish her goals of love and romance. Ursula pretends to be kind and caring, offering her land legs for three days with the condition that Eric fall in love with her/kiss her by the third day. The only thing Ariel has to do is sign her soul away and give up her voice. She gladly signs the contract and is whisked up to land with newfound legs. She is immediately rescued by Prince Eric himself, which would appear to be the ideal set up for success except for one thing: Prince Eric is in love with the girl who rescued him from drowning. If you're thinking "So far, so good," hold on for the twist of this mermaid 'tail' *(You had better be laughing again – out of delight or obligation. Either is fine).*

Eric only remembers/recognizes that girl by her voice.

Despite the obvious chemistry between them, and a whole lake full of sea animals delivering the clear instructions…

"Kiss. The. Girl."

…Eric remains oblivious, refusing to see what is right in front of him. His ears perk up however, when he hears the voice of his beloved coming from the sea witch in disguise.

All's well that ends well in the Disney version, as the necklace containing Ariel's voice is snatched away from the sea witch's throat, leading to the realization that Ariel was Eric's true love all along. Everything culminates in a grisly battle and a delightful nautical wedding.[8]

Such is not the case in Hans Christian Anderson's original tale. In that version, Eric marries someone else. The day of Eric's wedding dawns with a visit from Ariel's sisters. They have struck a bargain with the sea witch. If Ariel will kill Eric, the selfish prince who never noticed her presence or returned her love and allow his blood to drip on her feet she can be free of all bonds and return to her life in the ocean.

Ariel tries to do it. She does. Standing over the sleeping Prince Eric and his new bride, feeling the pangs of rejection and the ultimate twist of razor-sharp betrayal, she still cannot bring herself to end his life. She throws herself into the ocean, selflessly becoming sea foam instead.

*   *   *

I want love to look like rainbows and butterflies, tied up in pretty bows complete with bouquets of peonies and acrylic painting to memorialize the day. That's not always how it is.

Recently, I spoke to my friend Tyler during an altar service and reminded him of a conversation we'd had in the past:

> "Tyler, I came into the church this morning and I found myself overflowing with gratitude. I ended up weeping hysterically, I know you are surprised by this." (Tyler is not, in fact, ever surprised that I am weeping about anything). "I just remembered the conversation we had about a year ago. We were in the office, and I was just about to leave and you called me back and addressed a situation so boldly. You encouraged me to stay put, to grow from grace, and to exercise patience. I was so hurt, and broken, and

8 Disney's "A Little Mermaid"

bitter, but you told me not to speak defeat out of my mouth."

"But I am defeated," I said at the time, to which you replied.

"No. You are not."

"Today I couldn't help but cry and thank the Lord over and over again. Because you encouraged me not to give up, not to turn away in defeat, not to run and hide with my pain, to give grace, continue in patience, and lead with love, I have the most beautiful memories of the most beautiful moments. I kept thinking of incident on incident, joy on joy I wouldn't even have if I'd walked away."

"Your advice Tyler, it didn't give me all my dreams. It didn't get me 'girlfriend status', It didn't make me married. But it has made me more like Jesus."

* * *

It's not really the happy ending that counts the most, but how I practice His presence in the here and now. How much like Him I am.

Love puts on white dresses, sure. It carries bouquets, absolutely. But it is also longsuffering.

The word "love," means the willingness to suffer long, just as often as it means the privilege of dancing at a wedding.

It's ironic isn't it? The amount of time I spend writing about the futility of words.

It's ridiculous really… But bear with me.

It's just that I was thinking today of what it would be like, you know, to be Him. To come and live and breathe and walk perfect. *Perfect. (Note: walking perfect, doesn't guarantee you'll be wanted.)* There He was bruised and manhandled and waiting for sentencing. Waiting. Waiting for some sign that kisses don't always go hand-in-hand with outright betrayal. Waiting for a look of love from the people He created life for and gave His life to. Waiting for someone, *anyone* that He had poured Himself into, to speak up. And they did.

"Crucify Him."

Even political leaders were shocked by a choice that fickle; corruption that cruel.

"Really? Crucify Him? Wait. Here's a thought. I'll release a prisoner. I'll give you this guy you're all supposed to love or that scourge of society Barabbas."

"We'll take Barabbas."

Did they even blink beforehand?

The choice was so easy. And so very wrong. So there He was, about as pathetic as you can get. Stretched vulnerable and open wide *in front of, because of,* and *for the future of,* a crowd that jeered and spit. **Had they not *just* cried Hosanna?**

You know what guys? **He knows.**

That whiplash you get when someone who has spoken smooth words runs out of smart things to say and is a complete paralytic when it comes to action? He knows about that. Being passed over and forgotten so a once adoring audience can turn in a heartbeat to something straight up inferior? He knows about that too.

He had changed the whole world - and they kicked Him out of it.

He gets it - wanting to be loved as more than a lifeline. He understands it - getting so sick of being a catalyst because you just want to be a constant.

I get it too.

I'm sure that you are no stranger to some variation of

these feelings yourself, if you love God and have been trying to serve Him for any amount of time. People are usually involved in serving Him. To Him, people are the point and people, they up and choose Barabbas for no reason. I know this.

Not just because I know people. I know this because I am people. It devastates me to think of it. **How easy it can be to become addicted to how He makes me feel and how quickly I forget that He Himself has feelings.**

It's nice I'm sure. The high hallelujahs, the smooth words of praise, the whispered sentiments of love, and those triumphant and loud Hosannas. But that's not all He wants. He wants *me*.

He doesn't just want to bless my life, He wants to be a part of it. He doesn't just want me to *say* the right things but to *think* them and *do* them and *live* them. Because He *knows* in His heart of hearts, and all of His wisdom; **He knows**, that in the dark and in the silence when everything settles down **it's always Him or Barabbas**.

I told that platonic love of my life the other day:

"You won't do that. It requires too much emotional and physical effort and it would make you far too happy ultimately if you actually did it."

"You know me too well." he said.

It's not that I know him, it's that I know people. Because I am people. I don't know why it is that when we **know** it makes no sense, and we **know** that it is wrong, and we **know** it is not wise, and we **know** that ultimately, he will never make us happy, still…we choose Barabbas.

I am Judas and I am Jerusalem so much more often than I am ever Jesus.

What can I do but what we all do?

I try. I try to speak less, and live louder, and love longer, and be better. Even though I know it is an uphill climb, I'm trying. And when I say I love Him, you can be sure that I'm not lying. But words cost pretty pennies and unless you *live* them, no one's buying.

In the dark and in the silence when everything settles down, it's always right or wrong, light or dark, one or the other; Him or Barabbas. When I feel the pain of rejection, I know He is no stranger to it. When I want to give up on the people He's asked me to love, I remember He never gives up on me.

Grow from grace. Lead from love. Sacrifice self for the sanctity of His kingdom. It may not cause all your dreams to come true. It may not make you married. It for sure makes you a princess however, because it makes you more like Him.

16

WATCHING FOR WATER

The Trevi fountain is one of the most beautiful and well-visited destinations in the city of Rome. Pope Urban VIII charged a man named Gian Lorenzo Bernini to improve a pre-existing fountain in the year 1629. The death of the pope meant the project was abandoned, though some of the designs were grafted into the renovations which began to take shape in the following century.

Pope Clement XII hosted a contest to continue fountain renovations and a Roman-born architect named Nicola Savli won the grand prize of being able to take on the project. He began working on it in 1732, but died in 1751. The Trevi Fountain we see today was then completed by a man named Giuseppe Pannini.

I don't know about you, but when I see or hear the name "Pannini," it doesn't conjure up images of breathtaking fountains one would experience on Roman holidays, but rather of toasted sandwiches served with a side of chips. The man who did the majority of the work on the Trevi Fountain doesn't even get much of the credit. He's no longer living, but even if he were, it's my opinion that he wouldn't care. To know that thousands of people journey there annually to admire his handiwork and toss their hopes and dreams into it with the flick of coin after coin would likely be enough. Sometimes it's not about what you can see – your progress, your fortune, your name in lights

– but who sees you.

Tangled's Rapunzel doesn't even know that she's a princess. She's been stolen away from her kingdom and locked up in a tower until now, when Flynn Rider spirits her away for a daring adventure - her first in the real world. Every year she has watched the lanterns light up the sky on her birthday, inexplicably drawn to the beauty of the lights and wanting nothing more than to experience the splendor in person, outside of the confines of the cold walls of her tower. There, finally, she finds herself, floating along the river in a boat with the best looking man she's ever seen, as the lanterns take flight. She's finally experiencing the real world.

And as often happens in the "real world," the couple breaks into song:

> *"And at last I see the light,*
> *And it's like the fog has lifted*
> *And at last I see the light*
> *And it's like the sky is new*
> *And it's warm and real and bright*
> *And the world has somehow shifted*
> *All at once everything looks different*
> *Now that I see you"* [9]

I love that song. Of course I do. Doesn't everyone long to be seen... truly seen?

We've been discussing it lately; being "seen." One of my friends has worried that men only seem interested in her because she's beautiful. They never say

> "You're so smart."
> or
> "You're so wise."
> or

---

[9] Alan Menken and Glenn Slater for Walt Disney's "Tangled"

"You're so anointed."
or
"You're such a good person."
or
"You're kind to animals."

They seem focused solely on her outer beauty. No one seems to see her. (Ironically my own frustration seems to be the exact. polar. opposite. of this. Feel free to inject as much bitterness into that statement as you desire.)

The point is, I don't feel seen either. We rarely do.

Tammy Maltby says:

"Under all these reasons, all these motivations, I believe, is that deep desire to be seen. Really seen. To be fully, intimately known... and loved for who we are." Not what we look like. Not what we do. Not how we sound. Who. We. Are. **Loved**. For who we are.

We find Hagar in Genesis 16. She has been abused, impregnated by a man who is not her husband, slapped by Sarah, and is now wandering around in the desert. She is at the end of her rope, and this is a metaphorical rope mind you because she doesn't even own that much. Genesis 16 finds her on the backside of the sands of Nowheresville. Genesis 16 also finds God speaking. And while He does not relieve her of her pain or remove her from her situation (He sends her right back into the exact same problems actually) He does promise her hope, a future, and a light at the end of the tunnel:

> "The angel of the LORD found Hagar near a spring in the desert; it was the spring that is beside the road to Shur. And he said,
>
> 'Hagar, slave of Sarai, where have you come from, and where are you going?'
>
> 'I'm running away from my mistress Sarai,' she answered.

Then the angel of the LORD told her,

'Go back to your mistress and submit to her.' The angel added, 'I will increase your descendants so much that they will be too numerous to count.' The angel of the LORD also said to her: 'You are now pregnant and you will give birth to a son. You shall name him Ishmael, for the LORD has heard of your misery. He will be a wild donkey of a man; his hand will be against everyone and everyone's hand against him, and he will live in hostility toward all his brothers.' She gave this name to the LORD who spoke to her:

'You are the God who sees me,' for she said, 'I have now seen the One who sees me.' That is why the well was called Beer Lahai Roi; it is still there, between Kadesh and Bered,"

Genesis 16:7-14

It's Genesis 16:13 that catches my attention:

"You are the God who sees me. **I have now seen the One who sees me.**"

She names the water "God sees."

She calls her provision "God sees me."

She might as well burst into song:

> "All those days, chasing down a daydream
> All those years living in the blur
> All that time, never truly seeing
> Things the way they were
>
> And at last I see the light
> And it's like the fog has lifted
> And at last I see the light
> And it's like the sky is new
> And it's warm and real and bright
> And the world has somehow shifted
> All at once, everything looks different
> Now that I see you"

She goes back and submits to her situation in trust, knowing that God has seen her though nothing has changed.

Later, she's found in the desert again. Isaac is born. She and Ishmael are sent away.

> *"When the water in the skin was gone, she put the boy under one of the bushes. Then she went off and sat down about a bowshot away, for she thought,*
>
> *'I cannot watch the boy die.' And as she sat there, she began to sob. God heard the boy crying, and the angel of God called to Hagar from heaven and said to her,*
>
> *'What is the matter, Hagar? Do not be afraid; God has heard the boy crying as he lies there. Lift the boy up and take him by the hand, for I will make him into a great nation.' Then God opened her eyes and she saw a well of water. So she went and filled the skin with water and gave the boy a drink. God was with the boy as he grew up. He lived in the desert and became an archer,"*

Genesis 21:15-20 (NIV)

Her hopeless circumstance did not change the promise of God. There was water there, whether she could see it or not.

Dear Heart:

I wish you (I pray you) moonlit boat rides, sparkling lanterns, and romantic moments with that one - the one - who truly sees you, and loves you, and cherishes you for who you are. I wish you butterflies, and shivers, and knees like jello. But before you ever lock eyes with him, I wish that you lock eyes with the One who truly sees you. I hope the world shifts, and things make sense and that your love affair with Him lasts forever. Because it's the only love affair that truly can.

One of the best things about that kind of fairytale is that when you truly see the One who sees you, you start to see yourself better than ever before. You might even discover that your dreams can come true, that the lanterns were for you the whole time, and that you were a princess all along.

May your heart be hopeful, your hands be diligent, and your eyes be opened to see the wells were full of water all along.

17

TESTIFY YOUR DREAMS

"Testify your dreams." It was a specific phrase that came to me at early morning prayer. I knew I would be speaking to people in the near future, and the Lord was telling me to speak specific dreams, but not just to speak, to **testify** in gratitude for His faithfulness, in areas He had yet to move. He wanted me to speak aloud His greatness in places where life, just to be frank, was not all that great yet.

"What's the importance of that?" I wondered. "Why would I need to speak aloud the dreams He's given?"

This was a valid question. What was the correlation between the dreams He had given me and the importance of my speaking them?

I believe the answer to that can be found in 2 Corinthians 4:13.

> *"It is written: 'I believed, therefore I have spoken.' With that same spirit of faith we also believe and therefore speak,"* (NIV).

There are truths we think about, principles we harbor in our hearts, and to do so is one thing. Speaking it out, that's a different animal altogether. Perhaps, for example, I "believe" I am an author. It is one thing to think that statement and harbor it in my heart. It is another for me to speak it out of my mouth:

"I am leaving for Arkansas this week. I will be staying in the cutest Airbnb surrounded by a fence. Food will be delivered to the door of the house. Cows will moo and bellow at each other outside the house. But inside the house, I will stall and procrastinate, weep and cry and write. I will actually write a book. A whole book."

At the end of the day, if I really believe it, I will speak it. If I believe my dreams are from God, if I believe my promises are coming to pass, if I believe His Word is sure, I should have absolutely no problem testifying about that Word.

What does "testify" mean?

Testify: "To serve as evidence or proof of something's existing or being the case."[10]

Now…

What is faith if not the substance of things hoped for and the evidence of things not seen?

Hebrews 11:1

Testimony and faith go hand in hand. If I believe it, I will speak it. It's all evidence.

There's a delightful literary podcast I listen to on occasion called "The Lamppost in the Woods." It's produced by four friends, Evan Zenobia, Jennifer Malech, Benjamin D. Copple, and Dinah Copple. They have an episode called "Someday My Prince Will Come" which ironically has nothing to do with Snow White at all. It does, however, have a lot to do with the topic of dreams. They turn, in their discussion of dreams, to the stories of Cinderella and Joseph, two characters who are very different. One is male, one female, one is fictional, the other very real, one dreams of going to a ball and dancing with a prince and the other, in essence, of someday being a prince himself. I wouldn't

---

[10] Dictionary.com

normally put the two together, but when they do, it makes sense immediately. Cinderella does, after all, have dreams just like Joseph. In fact, she sings a song about it, a very popular and well-known song. You might have heard it, it's about dreams being a wish your heart makes:

A dream is a wish your heart makes
When you're fast asleep
In dreams you will lose your heartaches
Whatever you wish for, you keep
Have faith in your dreams and someday
Your rainbow will come smiling through
No matter how your heart is grieving
If you keep on believing
The dream that you wish will come true[11]

This poor girl lives in misery, works in sorrow, and hold on to hope that one day everything will be different. The whole story is full of ups and downs, twists and turns. She thinks she's going to the ball, then she doesn't get to go. She DOES get to go, becomes close to the prince, and then everything is ripped away. It all continues to go wrong until everything works out at the very last minute.

Joseph? He has dreams to, and he tells those dreams to his brothers which was admittedly and immediately a terrible mistake. I understand why he was excited. I've been excited too. Sometimes I'll get a dream I know is from God and run around excitedly yelling:

"YES! Pasture to palace!"

That's what I think it will look like. I assume Joseph also felt that way. I cannot fathom he ever realized his life trajectory would look much more like pasture, to pit, to Potiphar's house, to prison, and then to the palace.

---

[11] A Dream Is a Wish Your Heart Makes lyrics @ Walt Disney Company. Writers: Mack David, Al Hoffman, Jerry Livingstone, David Pack

Joseph does not have the privilege of being a Disney princess, but in the Dreamworks animated film "Joseph King of Dreams" he too sings a song:

> I thought I did what's right
> I thought I had the answers
> I thought I chose the surest road
> But that road brought me here
>
> If this has been a test
> I cannot see the reason
> But maybe knowing "I don't know"
> Is part of getting through
>
> I tried to do what's best
> But faith has made it easy
> To see the best thing I can do
> Is to put my trust in You
>
> For You know better than I
> You know the way
> I've let go the need to know why
> For You know better than I"[12]

The Lord, He allows us insight into undeveloped areas of our lives with dreams and promises. He gives us a glimpse of our future, and hope to hold on to, and the opportunity to develop trust in Him: To begin to understand that His ways are higher, to cultivate a faith in His Word and His way even when we don't understand it, to believe what He has to say enough to testify about it. We get a chance, every day, to take part in His great adventure.

Speaking of adventures, one begins in J.M. Barrie's Peter Pan with parents racing towards the nursery. While out at a dinner party they realize they have left the window open. Fearful for the future of their children they scramble to get

---

[12] "Better than I" from Joseph Kings of Dreams – Artist David Campbell

back to them in time. The narrator tells us:

> "It would be delightful to report that they reached the nursery in time but then, there would be no story."[13]

We all have that option. To be safe, but without a story. You have the option to retreat into your room and never risk or try or really live. You don't have to leave the window open. You don't have to let the light in. But the story He's telling is worth it, no matter what twists it takes you through.

I had seen myself on the platform of North American Youth Congress 2017. I had, in the Spirit, very clearly seen myself on the Youth Congress platform. I didn't know how it would happen, but I had seen it. Not long after, a friend suggest I try out for the North American Talent Search. I didn't love this idea. I didn't like that it was a competition. I hated putting myself out there. I wasn't a fan of the fact that it would be a performance. However, I had seen myself on the platform. I just had. I knew what I had seen.

So, I submitted a video. I wasn't picky about it, I didn't do as my friend encouraged me and really make the most of it and stand proudly saying my lines in various locations all over St. Louis or let them do fancy editing or videography. It was a half-hearted, one take, one frame sequence of me sitting at a coffee table, reading my words.

Inspired.

(Did you know if you don't try you cannot fail? Because I knew it. I have spent the greatest percentage of my life, so far, living like I don't know anything else.)

I paid the fee. I submitted the video. I dared to speak my dream out loud.

---

[13] Peter Pan by J.M. Barrie

I read the rejection e-mail over and over in an absolute fog of disbelief. I literally could not believe I hadn't made it. I was shocked, and my surprise had nothing to do with my ego or my belief in my own words. I was stunned at this rejection, not because of my belief in my skill, but because of the belief I had in what I had heard from God.

I was devastated, and about to head for Scotland, but I didn't want to go. I know, I sound like a crazy person because I was being given the opportunity to go to Europe (for free, I might add) and I didn't want to, but I am being honest with you, adventure did not appeal to me one bit. I wanted to stay safe and sound in my own house surrounded by my own things and not risk anything new ever hurting me ever again. I refused to pack. I refused to pack until the very last minute, then dragged my carcass reluctantly onto a plane praying I wouldn't be sorry I went.

I wasn't at all sorry I went. I would be lying to myself and you, however, if I did not admit in this moment that Scotland was a rough time. It was beautiful, impactful, life changing, and a time of pouring out in ministry, but it was also rough. That's just the way it was. It didn't matter much though because soon I found myself in a car with my best friend and our fathers, speeding away from Scotland to England. I felt the weight on my chest grow lighter with every mile we traveled and was overwhelmed with thankfulness for the beauty of the trip and the experience. There are not enough words available to a pen to express the importance of the people I was in the car with as we made the trip to Liverpool. I'm not just close to my friend Deandra, who married a Hemus, who swept her off to England like an actual real life princess, but I am close to her father as well. In addition to this, it was Father's Day weekend and I had not marked the occasion of that holiday in the actual presence of my own father for several years. The very air grew lighter as we journeyed along, and I found myself relaxing and beginning to enjoy the moment with every "thank you" I breathed out to God.

Days passed and my excitement mounted. We were going to take a trip to London. Just me, Deandra, and our friend Bernice. (Bean is a Ghanaian, relocated to England. Aside from being an overall delight as a person it was also such a breath of fresh air to be around someone who understood and embodied the customs, traditions, food, and inside jokes of the country I grew up in.) I, Melinda Poitras, who had been skulking around in defeat, just honestly, and blessed as I was, had not been excited about anything in a very long time. I was excited about London though. I would finally see the city I had dreamt about so often. I played the soundtracks to "Pocahontas Two: Journey to a New World", "What a Girl Wants", and (of course) Mary Kate and Ashley Olsen's "Winning London" on repeat the night before we were to leave. I could barely sleep. I felt all the anticipation of Christmas morning, and all the excitement of a brand new toy, rolled up into one.

We arose early and headed for the train station. A few short hours on my very first train landed us in London. Our first stop was to purchase tickets for the hop on, hop off, double decker red buses I had always dreamed of riding. We climbed to the top of the bus and snapped some photos, landing next to Ormond Hospital almost immediately. Great Ormond Street Hospital is significant to me as it is a children's hospital funded by the revenue still generated from J. M. Barrie's Peter Pan. I breathed in the busy magical air of London and listed off the things I cared most about in order: Visiting Shakespeare's Globe Theater, having a proper English tea, viewing Peter Pan's statue in Kensington gardens.

Here's the problem: The more of that busy magical air I breathed in the more I realized it was a lot less magical than merely busy. The temperatures were in the hundred degree region, Parliament was open, people were in the streets protesting recent apartment fires of some sort, and our double decker bus barely made it a block within the first hour of our riding on it. On the positive side, I really did get ample chance to take in every inch of the outside of the Great Ormond Street Hospital. The day had barely began and we were all wilting away. We didn't have the time to continue to wait for the traffic surrounding the bus so made the decision to purchase Tube tickets.

By the time we purchased tickets, made it down and up the various flights of stairs necessary, and I was packed onto the tube like a sea sick sardine attempting to eat tiny sustaining bites of croissant, I began to worry the day might not go as I had imagined it. If only I possessed the human capability to grasp just how badly it was about to go.

We finally got off the tube and made it up to the exit. As it turned out, the station closest to the Peter Pan statue was closed that day, and the second closest station was not at all close. Deandra blazed a trail ahead with relentless optimism and I (along with Bean) trailed behind her. My spirit wanted to rally and enjoy the day. My body quit on me. I don't know how to explain this to you other than to state that definitely and simply:

My body quit.

It was not playing. It would not be frolicking about for a happy day in London town, it would be checking out immediately.

If you have ever seen a photo of me, it will not shock you to read I am not a mountain climber. I'm not really into hiking. Or running. Or walking. Or standing. But quite honestly, I can hold my own. I had just left Scotland where me and my body were walking 18,000 steps a day. This was not an expected reaction. I did not anticipate this bodily mutiny, but like a rogue pirate on the Jolly Roger, mutiny became my body's middle name. Whether from the heat, the recent heartbreak I had weathered, the low state of my self-esteem, the lack of hydration, or the physical exertion of the trip as a whole I cannot say, but my body shut down. This is not an exaggeration. Time after time that day, I walked until I could not walk any more, collapsing into café chairs to drink multiple bottles of water, or into the grass on the side of the road. I couldn't even stand when we stopped. I would sink to the ground like a limp dish rag.

Deandra soldiered on. I did my best to follow her on this journey that was now taking hours of our time. My final collapse was intensely dramatic. She swore to me we were almost there and I informed her my body would not be joining her for one more step as I lay sprawled in the grass of the famous Kensington gardens. Bean wasn't fairing much better, to be honest, whether it was the heat of the day or her personal kindness to me I still do not know. Deandra left us both, saying she believed the statue was just around the corner.

She raced back, full of excitement. She had found it! I half crawled (Here you will be tempted to think me given to hyperbole. No. I literally crawled.) the few yards to round the clump of trees and there he was, Peter in all of his youthful glory.

I collapsed yet again onto a patch of grass next to the statue. (Here I know you will begin to sense a pattern from me. Collapsing from defeat is what I did on this trip.) No sooner had I done so, laying on the grass in public, not caring who saw my disheveled state or heard my labored breathing, than a man entered the courtyard.

"I am the crocodile," he said, addressing me. (There's a crocodile, I'm not sure if you know, who torments Captain Hook in the story. He's swallowed an alarm clock as well as Hook's hand and he chases him everywhere, sending the message that Hook will run out of time and the beast will devour the rest of him. What's more, there are also fabled and famed crocodile "river spirits" in the village of Paga, in Ghana, where I grew up.)

"I am the crocodile," he said. "Women are not meant to speak. **They are not meant to speak.** They have nothing of value to say. They need to remember above all else to keep their filthy mouths shut."

I was unsure of what was coming against me, and I was definitely too weary to combat it. I couldn't move my lips to formulate the name I needed, so I thought it, I closed my eyes and merely thought the name

"Jesus." Immediately that man snapped to attention and left. He walked quickly to the gate, paused, turned back to me, made direct eye contact and said:

"Fine. But You're ugly."

My two greatest fears:

1. I am not worth listening to.
2. I am not worth looking at.

The unhappiest of tasks fell to Deandra right around this moment. She was forced to tell me we would never make it to Shakespeare's Globe theater in time. I had come all the way to London, and hadn't gotten to see it. I ran to the nearest restroom and was violently ill. Then we, a rather dejected crew, stopped off for some proper tea (an experience I did get to have), purchased some souvenirs, and got back on the train to head for Liverpool. I had wasted our whole day in the endless hike to this statue.

We finally made it home, and Deandra took a shower while I sobbed, face down in the couch. I had journeyed to London only to arrive at the end of myself. This was the end of my trip. We had planned it in order to cap off the experience with a high point. So much for that.

I said goodbye to Deandra, not knowing when I would see her again, then boarded a series of trains back to Scotland by myself.

I reached the lowest point I have ever visited on that train to Glasgow. That wasn't all that happened on that train though. On that train, I yielded to the Lord. For the first time in my life I absolutely and fully surrendered. I realized:

> I *am not* worth listening to, but that's OK, because I want people to hear *Him.*

> I *am not* worth looking at, but that's OK, because I want people to see *Him.*

I let Him know it didn't matter how many random strangers threw things at me (three on that trip), or who I overheard talking about me when I left the room or the terrible things they said (on that trip), or how long it took me to wrestle away from the man who grabbed me and aggressively tried to solicit my services (on that trip although, I guess at least all the men in Europe did not find me repulsive?).

It didn't matter what anyone said or did or where they put their hands. I was going to go wherever the Lord wanted, I was going to love whoever He needed, I was going to speak to whoever He told me to, I was going to say whatever He said to say, whenever He said to say it, wherever He told me to say it.

Even if all of that happened again, and again, and again, I was His for sure, for certain, for life. I always told Him I would go anywhere but Europe. I don't think it was even about location. I think it was about how I put a "no" where He wanted a "yes."

I could have stayed home. I wanted to. I could have remained safe in St. Louis and nothing would have ever happened or changed. But then there would be no story.

I did go.

By the time I disembarked in Scotland, I had fully surrendered to the Lord.

* * *

In the timeline, I have arrived back in Scotland, but in reality we have not arrived at the craziest part of the story.

When I returned to the States, I gratefully collapsed into my own bed, only to be awaken by missed texts and voicemails beeping through. I had missed a phone call from LJ Harry. I wouldn't be a part of the North American Talent Search, but he had seen my monologue (which was no doubt flagged for him by my friend Tiffani) and invited me to share it in the early morning sessions of Youth Congress. I would, just like the Lord had showed me, be standing on the stage at North American Youth Congress 2017, but I hadn't received the voicemail, because I was journeying from England to Scotland.

The Lord launched my speaking ministry the day I decided I would never be intimidated into silence because I was willing to make His voice matter the most.

I would stand in the exact place He told me I would. Not because of my effort or skill or voice or looks but my surrender to the story and my willingness to leave the window open.

The story doesn't end there. I journeyed to Europe a second time that year, visiting the country of Greece. After a time of prayer my friend K came up to me. I hadn't told her about any of these experiences but she said:

"I saw you in Scotland. People were throwing things and being so hateful. I saw you in England and people were harming you with their words and I asked the Lord, 'Why is this happening?' He replied 'They are reacting to her that way because she looks so much like me.'"

"For no matter how many promises God has made, they are 'Yes' in Christ. So through Him the 'Amen' is spoken by us to the glory of God. Now it is God who makes both us and you stand firm in Christ. He anointed us, set his seal of ownership on us, and put his Spirit in our hearts as a deposit, guaranteeing what is to come."

2 Corinthians 1:20-22 (NIV)

Through Him are His own promises answered. Through Him I say Amen, I believe His word enough to say it out loud with my mouth.

Still. It's hard to testify your dreams sometimes. To look at this more intently, let's go back to the Lamppost in the Woods podcast (as we all should not just in this book but in real life. Seriously. Go check that out.). They make the point on that podcast that when Joseph testifies his dreams, his clothes are immediately ripped.

This also happens to Cinderella. She's never asked for anything and she's worked tirelessly and she's done her best her whole little life. Having scrounged together her own dress with the help of imagination and rodents she flies down the stairs breathless and beautiful and she says

"Wait! Wait for me! I'm coming to the ball!" This is the magical moment where her step-sisters rip her dress to shreds.

I don't know what it sounds like or looks like for you, maybe a little something like this:

- "We're going to have church in a stadium one day!" (Right before no-one is allowed to do anything in a stadium due to a global pandemic.)

- "I'm going to take him back! We stood at an altar. We said vows. He's the father of my children. I believe in his ability to do the right thing and make the right choices!" (Right before he sleeps with someone else again.)

- "I can't stop throwing up but I don't care because the pregnancy test was positive and I know that means this baby is developing, because this baby is going to be okay!" (Right before another miscarriage.)

- "I'm going to make moves and book tickets and walk in my calling!" (Right before the tickets sell out and the doors slam shut in your face.)

- "She's coming home, I've been praying for my baby and she's coming home!" (Right before she has to be checked into rehab.)

More often than not, it feels like that's how it is. Hold on though. Here's what happens:

Joseph goes through the pit, Potiphar's house, prison and then he lands in the palace. He continues to serve, continues to practice excellence, continues to thrive in character and one day, there his brothers are, kneeling at his feet. Joseph had lived his life for the Lord until he had forgotten what his former dreams were. I know that because it says, in Genesis 42, "Joseph remembered his dreams." He only even remembered his dreams when he was watching them come to pass in front of him.

You know why you can testify your dreams? Because nothing that happens in the middle of your story changes the ending.

You know how your story ends?
However He has said it would.

If He has said you're going to the ball, go ahead and break out your glass slippers. If He has said a palace is your destination – you will be living in one.

The beavers tell the children, when they slip through the wardrobe into Narnia and they are sharing the news of their ruler Aslan.

"He's not safe, but he's good." They tell them He is no tame lion, but he is trustworthy. This is the truth if ever I have heard it. I have tested and tried it and known it to be true.

He is not safe, but He is so so good.

Here's a final story from my travels (and travails) in 2017. One more encouragement and reminder to leave the window open:

No-one would have called him successful. He was a quiet, introspective child. When he grew up, he tried his hand at dealing art. Quitting that when his surroundings became depressing, he served as a missionary to Belgium for some time before returning home to live with his parents. His younger brother supported him financially and the two kept up quite the correspondence. He painted a lot. He drank a lot. He cut off his own ear. He spent some time in a psychiatric hospital or two. He killed himself.

On this foundation, much of the history of Western art is built. In roughly ten torturous years Vincent van Gogh produced 2,100 artworks, 860 of which are without question some of the best Post-Impressionist paintings ever imagined, one of which is my absolute favorite.

I love "The Starry Night". There are no rules to my arguably good taste. I might like something everyone loves or love something no-one likes, but whatever I'm fixed on I'm fixed on that. Hard. So when my friend Kristen and I were blessed to be at Women Ministering to Women in New York City there was just one thing we had to do. We **had** to go to the Museum of Modern Art (MOMA) and we **had** to see "The Starry Night". I had already gone all the way to London and not seen The Globe Theater (as you are well aware if you've made it this far) and I **was not** missing the opportunity to see this painting. No arguing. No questions. I had to see it.

Service ran long. (Thank the Lord. What a beautiful move of His presence we experienced that day.) We had to be on Broadway to pick up our Anastasia tickets at seven that night. The museum opened too late for us to make it the following morning without missing our flight. I had spoken that morning, and not eaten all day. (Because who has time for food? Obviously Jesus first, and then I'm trying to get to MOMA.)

To further complicate matters our beautiful tour guide Sarah, (whom we would have been HOPELESS without) had learned how to perfectly navigate the subway during the week, but the schedule changes on the weekends. It was hectic. I was hungry. The minutes ticked by, the trip was endless.

I looked across at Kristen and I told her:

"It's just a painting. It's just a thing. That's not even why we're here. I release this. It's okay. It will not ruin our night." But inwardly I stomped my foot and complained:

"I guess I am not meant to see any of the things I want to see in any of the cities I visit for ministry." Outwardly I cried a little.

We got off one subway line and hopped on to another. The minutes continued to tick by so Sarah and I decided we would all just get off at the next stop though we didn't even know what was there and Kristen and I would Uber to the theater.

Y'all. I was trying to be brave and I was trying to be fun but my heart was sad.

Y'all. We made our way onto the escalator and I looked to the right and the wall was plastered with posters that said "MOMA."

"Why do all these posters say 'MOMA' guys? Why? Why!?! Why!?!" I was not even pretending to be calm. When we exited that subway station the Museum of Modern Art was right. across. the. street.

We had twenty minutes. We booked it. Ran in. Bought tickets. Checked bags.

"Where's the Van Gogh ma'am? You know the one." We made it to the right level of the building. We couldn't find it. I was power walking past mesmerizing beauty all around us and could not locate the thing.

Kristen kept saying, "Just ask someone" and I kept snapping, "No. I need to find it myself. I need to find it myself!" because I was genuinely near hysteria. All at once we rounded a corner and time stood still as chill bumps crawled up my spine because there it was.

Kristen does a stellar dramatization of my original dramatic gasp. I'm not even ashamed of it. I did gasp. My knees buckled. Everything moved into slow-motion. I cried a little. It was so. much. better. in person.

I had thought about it. I'd seen pictures. I'd experienced prints. I'd noticed carbon copies on mugs and stationary and t-shirts but it was so. much. better. in person. I did not have all of the desired hours to read every plaque and gaze at every piece and commiserate with everyone standing next to me. It was not at all how I had planned it but there it was. Vivid, and vibrant, and moving. Not that it moved me emotionally, though it did, I mean it was moving on the canvas. Kristen had admonished me multiple times, knowing how I am:

"You cannot touch it."

I didn't have to touch it. It touched me.

This is one of the most beautiful moments I have ever had with the Lord. People faded. Sounds diminished. The lighting dimmed. I understood it. I understood all over again how very worthy of trust He is. How I can come to Him with my plans, and the desires of my heart, putting both of those things into His hands and trusting that He knows best: That His way is not only *right*, but *good*. Not just good for others, or the development of my character, or my ministry, but good for my heart as well. How trading my plans for His is never a bad deal, and ever the best decision.

He knows what He's doing, and when He does something it is always so. much. better. than I ever could have dreamed.

So I foresee, and I'm confident enough to state it, many starry starry nights ahead. I have an inkling that they'll be so much better in person. Besides, nothing in the middle of your story can ever change the ending He's planned. Go ahead and testify your dreams.

18

HAPPY ENDINGS
COME HELL OR HIGH WATER

My heart is full right now. It's full because no princess story is complete without a happy ending, and happy endings are really just beginnings anyway. Cinderella sings about it, in a little-known verse to "A Dream is a Wish Your Heart Makes."

> "A dream is a wish your heart makes, when you're feeling small, alone in the night you whisper, thinking no-one can hear you at all. You wake with the morning sunlight to find fortune smiling down on you. Don't let your heart be filled with sorrow, for all you know tomorrow, a dream you have wished will come true."

This song is very special to me. Once, I found a snow globe in a Hallmark store. It had the shoe from Cinderella inside of it, and was inscribed with the words "Even miracles take a little time." I sent it in the mail to a beautiful friend who I stood by, through a lot of heart ache. I ALSO stood by her on her wedding day recently, crystal shoe securely fastened into my gorgeous floral corsage pin. Here's something that can get a little confusing in the middle of your story; smack dab in the midst of the waiting:

> *"Now in this hope we were saved, but hope that is seen is not*

hope, because who hopes for what he sees? Now if we hope for what we do not see, we eagerly wait for it with patience,"
Romans 8:24-25 (NIV)

How on earth do we eagerly wait for something with patience? Is that an oxymoron? I thought about this for a while and prayed over it at great length, until I realized:

You can eagerly wait for something with patience, if you know that it is coming. Like a package in the mail, or a baby on the way. Which brings me to the story of my friend Sarah. My sweet Sarah had finally gotten pregnant with a baby she and her husband had been longing and praying for. It was a miracle in and of itself as doctors had given her a 3% chance of conceiving a baby naturally. We were thrilled at this news, but she miscarried. She miscarried her dream, and Mother's Day was fast approaching. I had been reading a book called "Waiting for Wonder: Learning to Live on God's Timeline" by Marlo Schalesky, and I knew it was time to give it to her. I bought some chocolate and packaged the book and wrote her a card and brought it to her on Mother's Day. When I asked her if I could borrow the book to look at it recently, she also still had the card.

Dear Sarah:

I know what it is like to want something with your entire being. I know what it's like to get it, only to have it inexplicably slip from my grasp. Most of all, I know what it's like to watch those closest to me get the very thing I wanted, and to be happy for them while wishing, just this once, we could all be happy for me... That, just this once, it could be my party, instead of me throwing another one. I do not know what it is like to love and lose a child I will never hold on this earth. I see you Sarah. Not just my beautiful friend who has experienced loss, but as a woman who has impacted the lives of so many children with patience, love, intelligence, and a sweet spirit. I see your kindness and your generosity. I don't know what emotions play through your mind this morning but overlooked must not be one of them. Because you are far from overlooked. Bible times were not short on mothers. But few of them are recorded, and even fewer made note of in that chapter of faith. Every child is a miracle, but none so much as that laughter child that came to Sarah, who waited. This book is terrible and I have been meaning to give it to you for months. I will sing your baby to sleep Sarah. But that moment we wait for is not what will make you a mother. You are one now, in so many ways that count.

I love you,
Melinda.

The very next Mother's Day, I got to give her a baby blanket instead. No-one knew she was pregnant yet, but I did. The doctor's note was mailed to my house, and I was the first person to see "It's a boy" scrawled onto that precious piece of paper. I do sing her baby to sleep. He's bilingual so I sing "Waymaker" in Spanish.

> *"Legacy is born in the waiting. It is built through God's work in the wait. Sarah taught me that. Her life shows me that God is most at work when I see Him the least."*

> Marlo Schalesky

Sarah wasn't the only one of my friends who was trying to have a baby. In the fall of 2019 I met up with my friend Lanae in Silver Dollar City. I will never forget dressing to meet her that morning because as I was getting dressed I looked in the mirror, and when I did, I saw us so clearly. I saw what she was wearing, the street we were walking on, I felt her link arms with me and tell me she thought she was pregnant. Later that day it all unfolded just as I had seen it. We walked down the exact street wearing the exact clothing I had seen. She linked her arm through mine and whispered

"I think I'm pregnant."

I couldn't believe the moment we were in and I teared up looking back at her to whisper

"I think you are too."

A pregnancy test confirmed the happy news and it was shared with much joy. A doctor's appointment brought bad news however. I was able to be with Lanae through the aftermath of some of that, but there was nothing I could do except sit. There were no words for this kind of pain.

She became pregnant again, and told her husband on Father's Day, by giving him a card he hadn't noticed her purchasing – even though he was right next to her. Joy was full, but this was followed by another miscarriage. I went to see her just after this one as well, and will not soon forget the feeling of putting my suitcase in the room intended for me and seeing all the baby paraphernalia coworkers had already given her. There would be no baby, yet again.

I was going through my own personal struggles at the time. I had seen in the Spirit, much earlier, a blonde baby girl. I knew her birth was tied to a change of life season for me. A change of life season I was desperately anticipating. I attended multiple gender reveals during this time, overjoyed my people were having babies, but distraught in my heart of hearts because every single child was a boy. I would sit in my car time after time, grateful we were having a beautiful new life but conflicted because I so desperately wanted things to change for me and here was one more sign that they weren't. I worried they never would. I cried a small lake. There are no doubts in my mind as to the scientific accuracy of this measurement of tear volume.

I don't know how all of this works. I don't understand why I would see a pregnancy but not anticipate a miscarriage. I don't know about the timing or the seasons or His ways which are higher than mine.

Here's what I do know. I know Lanae FaceTimed me in the Fall of 2020. We didn't have long to talk because it was a Sunday night and people were coming over for dinner but she wanted to tell me she was pregnant again. I thanked her for telling me, told her I loved her, and went about hosting my guests. At the end of the night, the one I call the Psalmist was the last to leave. I stood on the porch with him as rain began to fall. He was frustrated, because he hates rain as well as cold weather. I said

"No, no, no! We say, 'Thank you rain! We welcome you Fall!'" He was not convinced, nor would he repeat after me. Something happened in that moment on the porch though, I felt it. I physically felt the seasons changing.

I walked back into the house and shared the information I was not supposed to share with anyone, with my mother.

"Lanae is pregnant. She is pregnant. This baby will be fine, and it will be a blonde little girl."

The next day at prayer I read the verse in Jeremiah 5:28 which is describing rebellious people and it says "They do not say in their heart, Let us now fear the lord our God, who gives rain, both the former and the latter, in its season. He reserves for us the appointed weeks of the harvest." I wrote our names right there in my Bible. Right next to that verse. I texted Lanae and told her the seasons had changed, and I was going to acknowledge it with my heart and out of my mouth, long and loud. I also sent her the song "Your Nature" by Kari Jobe.

"You said you wanted a little girl, right?" Lanae said when she called after the doctor's appointment she had tried not to fear but still had been dreading.

"I said I had seen a blonde little girl that one time, but I obviously want whatever the Lord gives us. I will be just thrilled with a little ranch hand."

"Well, it is in fact a little ranch hand, but one you'll have to give princess lessons to."

She was pregnant with a perfect and perfectly healthy little girl who I have held in my own arms just a few short weeks ago. The day she was born her Aunt Lexie called just to double check:

"Mellie, I just wanted to make sure you saw that she's blonde."

I asked Lanae what kept her during some of this season, what held her together. She said often times it was songs she would listen to over and over. Specifically "Hell or High Water" by People and Songs. She's right. We would drive around listening to that song over and over. On my last visit, we listened to the song again, except this time when I made eye contact with her from the rear view the tears were happy ones. Her promise was sitting next to her in the back seat, nestled safe in a car seat.

When I left my visit to South Dakota to speak to the New York District ladies I told them all these stories. I showed them a picture of our promise girl. Then Charity, who is quite connected to the song "Hell or High Water" sang it over us as a congregation. There was a beautiful move of God's Spirit and such a sweet touch of His presence. On the way home I thought of friends I have prayed with for a baby. Friends who have been waiting a long time. I prayed over them again. Within the week two of them let me know they were pregnant.

So there I was, standing in a Hallmark shop once again. An attendant walked up to me and said, unsolicited:

"Have you seen these?" I turned and stared into the most adorable display of Baby Yoda baby gifts dreamed up under heaven. There were plush toys, swaddle blankets, and a snow globe that said, "A child is the greatest adventure in the galaxy."

I had left church in the middle of service to get my friend a Father's Day card last year. This year, by Father's Day, his wife was pregnant at long last. They both love Star Wars. I hadn't said a word when I turned to look at the Hallmark store worker. She looked back at me with a confused expression:

"I have goosebumps! I mean," and she showed me her arm, "Look! I have goosebumps."

As she rang up the second Hallmark Disney themed snow globe I have purchased in my life I told her she had goosebumps because the Lord is faithful. He not only makes dreams come true, He surpasses them, even if the miracle does take a little time.

> *"Now to him who is able to do immeasurably more than all we ask or imagine, according to his power that is at work within us"*
>
> Ephesians 3:20 (NIV)

> *"Looking unto Jesus, the author and finisher of our faith…"*
>
> Hebrews 12:2 (NIV)

I don't know how far today finds you from your happy ending, but I know you can trust your story. I know that, because I know who is writing it. Know the author. Trust the story. Break out of disappointment for you are held, come hell or high water.

ABOUT THE AUTHOR

Melinda D. Poitras

Melinda was born in Alabama, raised in Ghana, and currently lives in St. Louis, Missouri. She has been many places and is grateful that God is the same in all of them. She lives to promote His name and fame in any and every possible way. Writing is her favorite way.

Someone wise once told her that if she would write, it would enable others to run. That's what she wants to do more than anything: enable others to run. So, she writes what she can from her *own* heart, ever praying that the Lord take them and turn them to fuel for someone else's.

And the LORD answered me, and said, Write the
vision, and make it plain upon tables,
that he may run that readeth it.
Habakkuk 2:2